A PIONEER WORKSHOP

A PIONEER WORKSHOP

by
Judy Slaughter Cole
and
Mary Mitchell Minturn

Illustrated by
Grayson Slaughter

The Lowell Press
Kansas City, Missouri

FIRST EDITION

© Copyright 1975, by Judy Slaughter Cole and Mary Mitchell Minturn

Printed in the United States of America, 1975
Library of Congress Catalog Card Number 75-24614
ISBN 0-913504-26-2

The John Wornall house

FOREWORD

The Wornall House, completed in 1858, is Kansas City, Missouri's only restored house museum, and is known to be one of the best documented ante-bellum homes in the country. It is the setting of the 1858 Workshop which conducts classes for children in activities of the 1800's. You might say that the projects in this book are "tried and true," because after trying them and modifying them over a period of three years, we have found that these are the projects that the children liked most.

*Dedicated
to
Mary Pat Abele*

and to all of the children who have shared in the experiences of the 1858 Workshop.

ABOUT THE AUTHORS

Judy Slaughter Cole has been the Director of the 1858 Workshop at the Wornall House since its beginning in 1973. Her educational background includes study at Connecticut College and the University of Kansas where she earned her Bachelor of Science degree in Elementary Education. Her teaching experience has spanned pre-school through fourth grade levels. She has conducted workshops for teachers at a community college and at the Learning Exchange of Kansas City. Judy's interest in history was sparked by long conversations with a remarkable grandfather, and heightened by the discovery of eleven years of family diaries from the 1800's.

Mary Mitchell Minturn, mother of two sons, and teacher in the Shawnee Mission Public School system lives in Fairway, Kansas. She received a Bachelor of Science degree in Elementary Education and Family and Child Development from Kansas State University. She is presently working towards her Graduate Degree in Education. Her previous teaching experience includes Head Start and various grade levels in Illinois and Texas. During the summers, Mary has researched and taught history-related projects for children at the Wornall House. Her love of history stems from listening to the Laura Ingalls Wilder books read to her by her parents and teachers.

ABOUT THE ILLUSTRATOR

Grayson Slaughter, a student at the Academy of Art in San Francisco, has lived in Vermont, New York City, Europe, and Kansas City. Although he has held a wide variety of occupations, he considers illustration to be a permanent part of his life. His work includes illustration for the Westchester County Public Library young adult newspaper, set design for the New York City Public Theatre, and tri-annual brochures for the Wornall House.

Special thanks to Murray Gushka for the typography on the cover and chapter heads. It is a wood-engraved type dating from the mid 1800's.

CONTENTS

Foreword v
About the Authors vii

TOYS AND DOLLS
    Apple Head Pop-up Puppet 3
    Jumping Jack 5
    Moon-Winders 6
    Wooden Spoon Dolls 7
    Jacob's Ladder 8
    Clothespin Dolls 10
    Corn Husk Dolls 11
    Helpful Books 14

GAMES
    Who Goes First? 19
    The Wonder Puzzle 20
    Graces 21
    Hide the Thimble 22
    Hop, Step, Jump 23
    Table Football 24
    Witch in the Jar 25
    Helpful Books 26

INDIAN CRAFTS
    Signs and Symbols 29
    Owner Stick 32
    Indian Rattles 34
    The Bowl Game 35
    Sand Painting 36
    Clay and Kilns 37
    Indian Trail Signs 40
    Helpful Books 41

PIONEER COOKING
    Funnel Cake 45
    Mahala's Apple Dumplings 46

Salt Water Taffy 47
Johnny Cakes 48
Toasted Pumpkin or Squash Seeds 49
Carmel Corn 50
A Milk Carton Ice Cream Machine 51
Jennifer's Gingerbread Mix 52
Peach Leather 53
Helpful Books 54

SEWING, WEAVING AND DYEING
Embroidery 57
Appliqué 60
Patchwork 61
Wool
    Carding 64
    Spinning 64
    Dyeing 65
    Weaving 67
Helpful Books 69

HOLIDAYS
Valentine's Day 73
Easter 77
Independence Day 80
Apple Day 84
Halloween and Pumpkin Day 88
Thanksgiving and Corn Day 92
Christmas 96
Helpful Books 100

BITS AND PIECES
Candles 107
Rose Pot Pourri 108
Stenciling 109
Soap Making 110
Crystalized Violets 111
Peach Sticks 112
Home Comforts 112

Toys and Dolls

APPLE HEAD POP-UP PUPPET

History: Children often made their own toys from materials that were close at hand. Apples were plentiful in the autumn even if you had just one apple tree. So while mother prepared them for winter storage, the children could have fun carving apple heads. These dolls have been known to keep for years even though they are made from perishable material.

Procedure: Find a *big, hard apple* like a Jonathan, Winesap or Delicious. Using a *knife,* peel the skin leaving a little at the top and bottom so that it will dry in a round shape. Carve the features, but not very deeply. Remember that since the apple will shrink to half its size, the features should be far apart.

Put your apple head on a *dowel stick* three-eighths inch in diameter and twelve inches long where the air can circulate around it. Leave it for three or four weeks.

As it grows older you may pinch and pull it to change the face if you like. *Cloves, beads, felt tip pens, cotton* or corn silk, and wire for glasses are materials you might use for decorating the face.

Make a funnel from a half circle of *poster board* eleven inches in diameter. Overlap the edges an inch and *staple* in place leaving an opening in the bottom for the stick to go through. Cut a strip of *fabric* seven inches wide and fourteen inches long. You might choose calico or tiny checks for a sunbonnet grandmother or blue denim for a cowboy or an engineer. Staple the long edge around the funnel top overlapping the two short edges where the funnel is stapled together. Use a *needle* and *thread* to gather the top edge.

Put your stick with the apple head on top through the neck gathers and out the bottom funnel hole. Glue the stick inside the head with *white glue* for durability and inside the neck gathers to hold them in place. You can add *buttons* or *lace* or a *bow tie* for decoration. Two *felt* mittens glued to the fabric will complete your puppet.

Now you are all set to have fun making your puppet pop up, look in all directions, and then disappear again into the funnel.

For younger children: An adult may peel the apples for the children and let them make indentations with scissor points for the features. You only need to make two holes for eyes, slits on either side for a nose, and a slit for the mouth. Believe it or not this will make a shriveled face that can be molded as it dries. Mount the apple on a dowel stick, insert cloves for eyes, and follow the directions for making the clothes of a spoon doll. (See Wooden Spoon Dolls in this chapter.)

Related Activities:
1. Find out something about the everyday activities of people during a period in American history. Plan conversations between two or three puppets which reflects this period. Take turns presenting the conversations to others.

2. Find out what causes old people to have more wrinkles than young people.

3. Discuss the role of older generations in America one hundred years ago and now.

JUMPING JACK

History: A forerunner of this toy was popular in France over two hundred years ago and was then brought to this country. Although the pasteboard doll was intended for children, it became a favorite toy of the French court where it depicted shepherds, famous people, and jesters. In America the traditional forms have been Jack, a man, and the egg-shaped Humpty-Dumpty.

Procedure: Using *crayons* or *felt tip pens* draw arms, legs, and a body with a head attached on *cardboard*. Make the arms and legs longer than you want them to appear because part will be hidden behind the body. Using *scissors,* cut out the pieces and then make two holes at the body end of the arms and legs with a *hole punch*. Fastern *brads* loosely through the outside holes of the arms and legs. This will let the legs and arms move easily. Thread *string* through the holes as shown and tie the ends together. (Illustration) By holding the head and pulling down on the string, your Jumping Jack will jump.

Back view

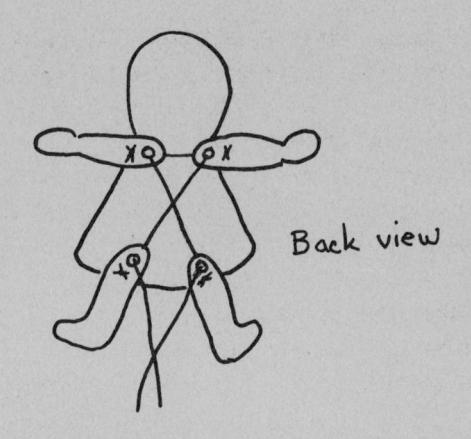

Related Activities:
1. Try making your favorite sports figure, dancer, circus character or animal.

2. Paste on clothes and hats made out of colorful material scraps. What could you do with feathers, beads, buttons, and yarn?

3. Make Uncle Sam celebrating the Bicentennial when he jumps up and down.

4. What was happening in France two hundred years ago? What was Benjamin Franklin's connection with France? What is the significance of the Statue of Liberty?

MOON-WINDERS

History: Discs of wood and common buttons were used to make the moon-winder. This toy is sometimes called a buzz saw because of the whirring sound it makes. School boys were known to buzz them into the hair of a girl sitting in front of them making a snare in her long locks.

Procedure: Here is a method of making a cardboard moon-winder. Using a *compass,* make a circle four inches in diameter from *corrugated cardboard* at least one wall in thickness. Cut it out with *scissors* and center two holes about a half inch apart and as wide as the *string* that will go through them. Accurate centering is important for balance. The string should be heavier than kite string to withstand the pulling and twisting and it should be cut thirty-six inches long. Thread it through one of the disc holes and back through the other tying the string ends.

Hold the moon-winder by hooking your index fingers through the loops of the string. Begin the motion by flipping the disc over several times. Then by alternately pulling and slackening the string, the disc will increase its speed.

Related Activities:
1. Punch eight holes uniformly around the rim of a cardboard disc to increase the buzzing sound. Why does this work?

2. Paint alternate dots of blue and yellow in a circle around the disc. What color appears when the disc spins?

3. Saw pine discs from a discarded Christmas tree and drill two holes in the center for another type of moon-winder.

WOODEN SPOON DOLLS

History: Through the centuries and in every culture little girls have had their dolls. In early America the pioneer children found it necessary to use the items around them and a little imagination. Often times, mothers were so busy with household chores that they could not stop to make a cuddly rag doll. The children soon found that a doll could be made from a simple wooden spoon.

Procedure: With *paint* or *felt tip pen,* make a face in the rounded part of a *wooden spoon. Buttons* make nice eyes and *yarn* or *cotton* hair could be added. The dress or pants could be made out of *fabric* or *paper.* Scraps of *lace, rick-rack,* and *felt* make charming additions and give your doll real personality. *White glue* works nicely for adding the extra features. Use your imagination!

Related Activities:
1. Make a puppet stage from a cardboard box and use your spoon dolls as characters in a play.

JACOB'S LADDER

History: This toy has mystified children for generations. Its name comes from the climbing and tumbling motion created when the top two blocks touch each other. The name Jacob's Ladder comes from the Bible, Genesis 12:28.

Procedure: Cut seven squares of *hard wood* each measuring 2½ x 2½ x ¼ inches. Cut a piece of *twill tape* ¼ inch wide and one hundred and eight inches long. Lay all squares end to end making a train effect. The blocks may be decorated before the twill tape is added. (See the Related Activities at the end of this project.) Fasten the twill tape between the blocks in an alternating fashion. The outside pieces of tape lay over the first block and behind the second block. The tape is fastened to the top of the wooden square with *small tacks* or *headed nails.* If the two outside tapes are on top, the center tape is underneath. The center tape is always tacked on the bottom of the block. (Illustration.) Each block should be as close to the next one as possible. Each block of wood has two strips of twill tape nailed to the top edge and one strip of twill nailed to the bottom edge.

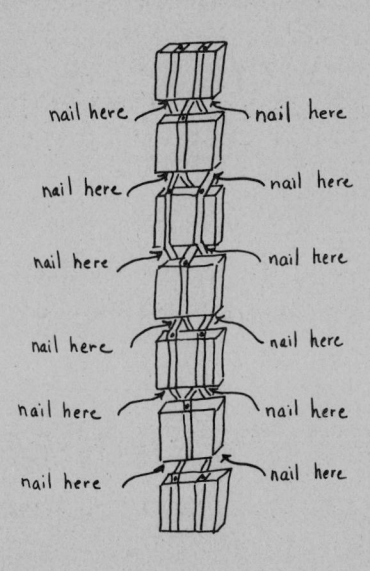

nail here   nail here
nail here   nail here
nail here   nail here
nail here   nail here
nail here   nail here
nail here   nail here

Start the tumbling effect of your finished Jacob's Ladder by holding the top block in your hand. Lay it over the second block and it will begin to tumble. You always have a grip on the top block. Turn your wrist in an up and down motion to keep the action moving.

Related Activities:
1. Try decorating each block with pictures of people or events in history. Alternating quilt designs could be done with actual pieces of material glued to the wood pieces, or the design could be transferred with a felt tip pen.

2. Try putting a bright piece of paper behind the first

two strands of tape. As the ladder moves, the paper appears and disappears. Is it actually moving from front to back of the wood block?

3. Have fun with fractions by changing the dimensions of the square and figuring the amount of wood needed for the seven blocks.

CLOTHESPIN DOLLS

History: Girls and boys alike will delight in the historical characters that can be made quickly from a wooden clothespin. Ladies, gentlemen, grandmothers, Indians, cowboys, and early settlers can be fashioned with a slight change in costume.

Procedure: Start with a *round wooden clothespin* three to four inches long. Flatten the face area with a piece of *sandpaper* and add eyes, nose, and mouth with *paint* or a *fine tipped felt pen. Yarn* or *cotton* can be used for hair. Wrap a fat *pipe cleaner* around the body right below the head area. This will form the arms and hands. Clothes can then be added to complete the character desired. Below is a versatile pattern for a shirt. Seams may be closed with *white glue* or you may actually sew them.

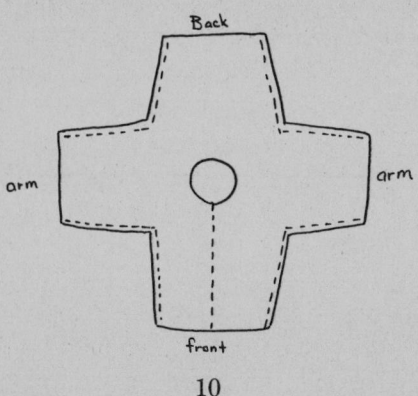

Legs can be painted for men and skirts can be added for ladies. Here is a basic skirt pattern.

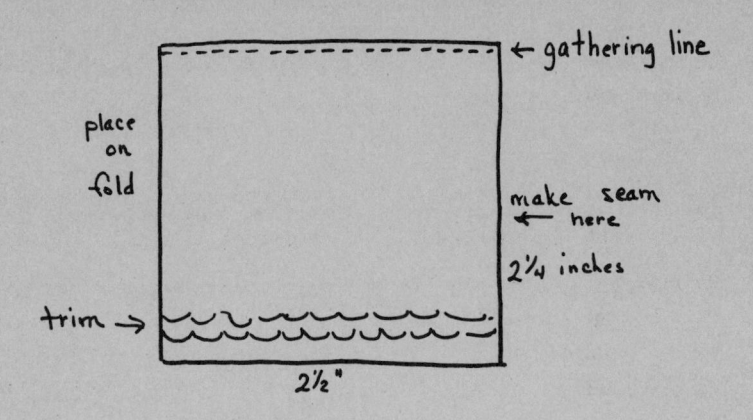

(diagram of skirt pattern: "← gathering line", "place on fold", "make seam ← here", "2¼ inches", "trim →", "2½\"")

Related Activities:
1. Try making a frontier town for your dolls. Start the buildings with odd shaped boxes. Children could be made with tiny wooden clothespins in a similar fashion. (For smaller clothespins, look at dimestores in the children's toy department.)

CORN HUSK DOLLS

History: Corn husk dolls are one of the oldest forms of dolls known to Americans. These dolls were first made by the Indians. The Iroquois tell the legend of the "faceless doll." The first corn husk doll was made as a playmate for a young Indian girl, but the doll was so beautiful that she spent all her days looking at herself in a clear pond in the woods. The Creator punished the doll for her vanity and removed her face forever.

Procedure: You can prepare your own *corn husks* rather than buying them from a craft supply store.

Lay them out on a *newspaper* or put them in a *mesh laundry bag* and hang them where the air can circulate through them. This will take about two days during which time they will curl and shrivel. They will return to their natural size and shape when soaked in water. If the husks become spotted and molded during drying, add a small amount of *liquid bleach* to the soaking water.

The husks should be soaked in *warm water* a total of thirty minutes before working with them. When they are soft and pliable, gather six corn husks at the large end, holding the tips down. About one inch from the top, wrap a tight *string* around all six husks. You could try the old-time method of using a thin strip of corn husk in place of string. Now cut off the top one-half inch and turn the husks down over the knot. (Illustration number one) This forms the head and hides the starting point of your doll.

After all of the husks are pulled down over the knot, wrap a piece of string around to form the head. (Illustration number two).

(1)

(2)

Form the arms by rolling husks lengthwise and tie each end to form the hands. (Illustration number three).

(3)

Now fit the arm piece under the head between the six husks. (Illustration number four).

(4)

Tie a string under the arms to form the waist. Criss-cross the chest area with two thinner husks, pulling the husks tight and tying the ends of the strips down at the waist with another piece of string. This gives a shoulder effect to your doll (Illustration number five). A longer skirt may be added by laying corn husks over the waist strings making the skirt fuller and fuller.

(5)

Cover the strings and rough waist edges with a small strip of husk. Now cut the husks off even at the bottom so that the doll can be free standing. A string tied loosely around the skirt will help it hold its shape while drying. Add *corn silk* for hair and a *fabric* bonnet and apron. Arms can be molded while the husks are wet. String support can be used until the arms are completely dry. Be creative and give your doll real character.

Related Activities:
1. A corn husk man may be made in the same manner separating the skirt into legs and wrapping the legs with another husk. He may be in a sitting or standing position.

2. Angels and birds may be made from corn husks and are less complicated than the dolls. You will find these explained in *Corn Husk Crafts,* by Margery Facklam and Patricia Phibbs.

3. Try using a natural dye to add color to your husks (See Sewing, Weaving, and Dyeing chapter).

Helpful Books for Dolls and Toys

American Folk Toys, Dick Schnacke, G. P. Putnam's Sons, New York, 1974.

Corn Husk Crafts, Margery Facklam and Patricia Phibbs, Sterling Publishing Co., Inc., New York, 1968.

How to Make Cornhusk Dolls, Ruth Wendorff, Arco Co., New York, 1968.

Mountain People, Mountain Crafts, Elinor Horowitz, Lippincott, 1974.

Early American Toys, Ginny Graves, The Learning Exchange of Kansas City, Mo.

Peepshow into Paradise, Lesley Gordon, John De-Graff, Inc., New York.

Games

© 1975 Grayson Slaughter

WHO GOES FIRST?

History: In the mid 1800's children had many jingling rhymes that they repeated to decide who in the group would go first in a game. These rhymes were called "modes of precedence."

Procedure: One of the players repeats a jingling rhyme. Each time he says a word, he points to a different player starting over again in the same order when he finishes going around once. The person who is pointed to last is the one to go "out" from the group and be "it." These are two of the most popular ones:

>Heater, beater, Peter mine,
>Hey Betty Martin, tiptoe fine,
>Higgledy-piggledy, up the spout,
>Tip him, turn him round about,
>>One, two, three;
>>Out goes he!

>One-ery, two-ery, hickory Han,
>Phillisy, follisy, Nicholas John;
>Spinkum, spankum, winkum, wankum,
>Twiddlum, twaddlum, twenty-one.
>>O-U-T, out,
>>With a white dish-clout — out!

Related Activities:

1. Use your imagination to write a story explaining the meaning of the rhymes. Make up a poem using your own nonsense words. The fantasy world of *The Adventures of Alice in Wonderland* came alive because of Lewis Carroll's use of nonsense words.

2. Make up a game where someone has to be "it" and you can choose him by using a jingling rhyme.

THE WONDER PUZZLE

History: Monthly magazines such as "Godey's Lady's Book" and "Peterson's Magazine" were full of things which were interesting to the lady of the house. They included serialized stories, recipes, home remedies, parlor games and directions for such projects as drying flowers. Puzzles were a popular pastime. A puzzle or riddle would be printed one month with the answer printed the following month. Here is a fascinating one:

Procedure: Here is the way the problem was stated in "Peterson's Magazine" in 1854. "Cut a piece of cardboard five inches by three inches so that you may pass through it, yet preserving it in one piece." In other words, figure out how you can make a five inch by three inch piece of paper big enough to put your whole body through it. You may make cuts in it, but you must keep it in one piece.

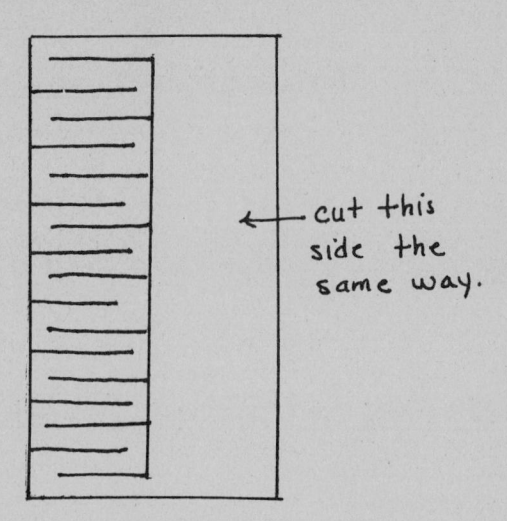

← cut this side the same way.

Here is how it is done. Fold a five inch by three inch piece of *light-weight cardboard* lengthwise down the middle. Using *scissors* cut a slit on this fold leaving one-fourth inch of one of the five inch edges. Move one-fourth inch over and cut from the outer edge to within one-fourth inch of the center slit. Repeat this process until you have cut both halves of the cardboard in this manner. Expand the paper by pulling outward. Step through it.

Related Activities:
1. Make an expanded paper circle by folding a paper circle in eighths and cutting first from one direction then from the other as you did in the Wonder Puzzle.

2. Make up a paper puzzle and write down the solution, explaining it clearly enough so that someone else could understand.

3. Use one-half inch cuts instead of one-fourth inch and measure the difference in expansion.

GRACES

History: In the 1860's this was a popular game played indoors with small hoops and sticks. Then it was only considered proper for a boy to play it with a girl as his partner. Some American Indian tribes played a version of this game.

Procedure: Use a smooth, sturdy *hoop* about twelve inches in diameter. This may be wood, plastic, or metal and it must hold its shape. Each player needs two *dowel sticks* three feet in length.

The hoop rests on the crossed sticks until they are forced apart quickly causing the hoop to fly into the air. A partner may catch the hoop on his two crossed sticks.

Place left hand here →

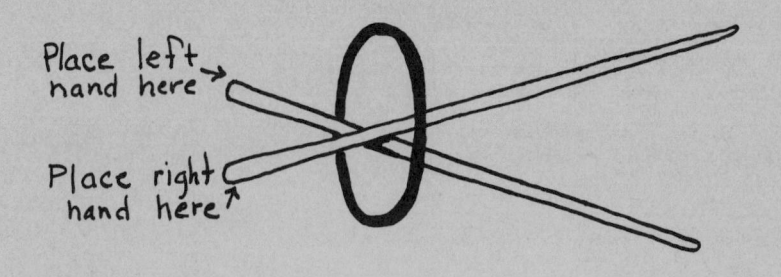

Place right hand here ↗

Related Activities:
1. Partners may play with two hoops throwing them at the same time and catching them.

2. With feet on a starting line, throw the hoop from your sticks as far as you can and have a partner mark the landing spot. See who can throw it the farthest. Measure the distances that you and your friends throw the hoop and graph the results.

3. Use a stop watch to see who can keep the hoop in the air the longest.

4. Try playing an Indian variation of this game by putting a hoop on the ground and stepping away several steps. With your back to the hoop try to toss the sticks into the circle.

HIDE THE THIMBLE

History: Children have a heritage all their own in the games and rhymes that are passed from one generation of children to the next. Hide the Thimble is an example of a game that has actually passed through centuries. It is easy to imagine a colonial child borrowing his mother's thimble to play this game inside with brothers and sisters on a cold New England winter day.

Procedure: One person hides the *thimble* while the others are out of the room. It must be within view, but not easily seen unless pointed out. As the players return they walk around the room silently looking for the thimble. When a child discovers the thimble he calls out "Rorum torum corum," and sits down. The others who are still looking may be helped out by the seated players who tell them, "You're freezing," "You're cool," "You're burning up," depending on how close to the thimble they are. The one who finds it last, hides it next.

Related Activities:
1. It may be interesting to find out *how* our heritage is passed from one generation to the next. We do not have to learn about songs, and games, and manners by reading about them in a book.

HOP, STEP, JUMP

History: Children had to devise games using little or no equipment because they had few manufactured toys available then. They relied on their imaginations to think up games using what was close at hand. This game was designed for boys, since girls were to remain dainty and lady-like.

Procedure: All the players stand behind a starting line. Each player needs a *small, marked stone* to mark his completed position. Each child hops, landing on one foot, balancing until he can take a big step with his opposite foot. He then brings up his back foot, and then jumps with both feet together. The winner is the player who can go farthest after one hop, one step, and one jump.

Related Activities:
1. Try the game with one slide, one skip, and one gallop.

2. Try measuring your distance using the metric system.

3. Find out about the first women to have participated in previously all-male sports. What sports are these? Are there still some that are all-male?

TABLE FOOTBALL

History: American children before the twentieth century had no television or other electrical appliances to keep them entertained. They had to devise games which would be active yet could also be played inside. Here is an exciting game.

Procedure: The players stand around a rectangular table with their captains. Boundaries are marked with *chalk* or *tape*. A line is marked in the middle of the table as well as about three inches from each end of the table to show the goal line. A *blown egg* is then placed on the middle line. The signal is given by the referee and the members of each team blow the egg towards their goal lines at the opposite ends of the table. No player may leave his place and the "football" must be moved entirely by blowing.

Using other rules.... a child gets five blows to see what his total score will be. No score is added if the egg stops on a line or falls on the floor. The winner is the player with the highest score after five consecutive blows.

```
┌─────────┐
│   20    │
├─────────┤
│   15    │
├─────────┤
│   10    │
├─────────┤
│    5    │
├─────────┤
│  egg ●  │
└─────────┘
   ↖ Player stands here
```

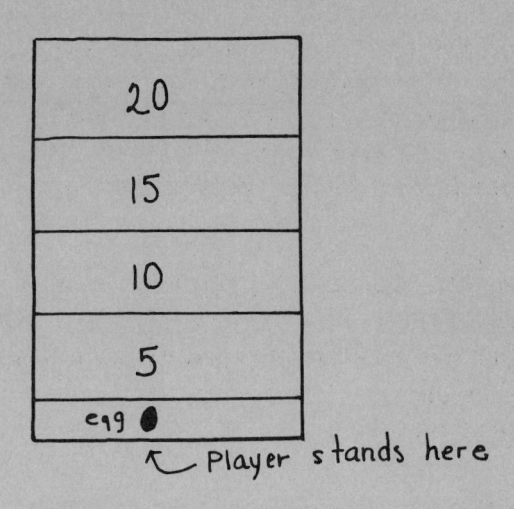

Related Activities:
1. It might add to the excitement if each team picked a name such as the "Yale Bulldogs," and a cheering section made banners for their favorite teams.

2. Enlarge upon the rules of this game. Could regular football rules be applied?

3. Another variation of the game is called "Blowing Eggs." One blown egg is needed and a long table. The table should be marked off as the diagram below shows.

WITCH IN THE JAR

History: It is difficult to find the exact beginnings of certain games such as Witch in a Jar, but it is probable that this game was made up because of the great excitement over witches in the seventeenth century in this country. Salem is the name of a very old town in Massachusetts which is identified with the history of witches.

Procedure: A witch is chosen who then draws circles on the ground which become jars to hold the players that she catches. The other children each find a rock or tree for their home. They can use this as a base from which to taunt the witch and then run back to safety. When the witch catches a player, she puts him in a jar. A player may not escape from a jar unless he is tagged by a free player. Once he is freed, he cannot be caught again until he has touched his base and leaves it again. The witch can catch the one who set him free, though. The last one to be caught becomes the witch for the next game.

Related Activities:
1. It would be easy to change the names in this game and still keep its structure. For instance, near Thanksgiving time you could have a farmer trying to catch his turkeys to put them in pens. Think up variations for any occasion or holiday.

Helpful Books for Games

1. Home and Child Life in Colonial Days, ed. Shirley Glubok, Macmillan Co., N.Y., 1969.

2. The American Boy's Book of Sports and Games, pub. Dick and Fitzgerald, 1864, N.Y.

3. Games for Everybody, May C. Hofmann, Dodge Pub. Co., N.Y., 1905.

4. "Early American Life" magazine, pub. Early American Society, Volume VI, Number 4, August 1975.

Indian Crafts

© 1975 Grayson Slaughter

SIGNS AND SYMBOLS

History: The signs and symbols of early American tribes tell a story of events and wars as well as tribal history. The symbols were painted with bright colors made from dried and crushed weeds, grasses, and flowers and mixed with water. Most symbols are self explanatory. For example, a buffalo is simply pictured as a buffalo. A more abstract symbol might be the word "peace," which is shown as a broken arrow, since no one could fight with a broken arrow.

Procedure: Use a blunt *pen* and *India ink,* or a *small brush* in *tempera* for best results.

Indian representation of five white men

Camp or village

Medicine or herbs

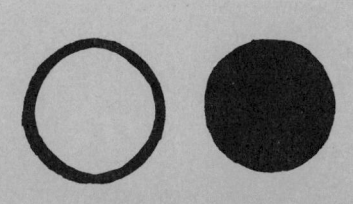

Life and death

Good drinking water here

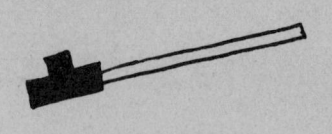

Peace pipe—sign of friendship

Love—the heart is within a circle

The eagle feather represents honor

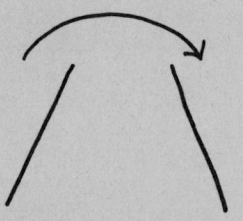

Across or beyond

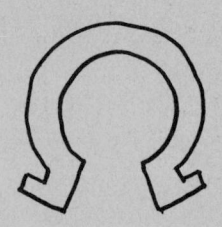

White man's horse (horseshoe)

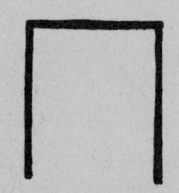

Indian's horse (hoofs weren't shod)

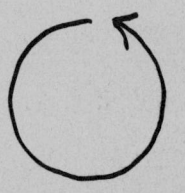

All or everyone

Three days

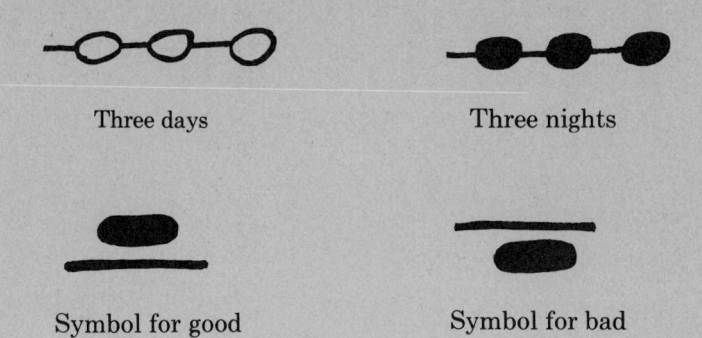

Three nights

Symbol for good

Symbol for bad

Related Activities:
1. The Woodland Indians scratched or etched their symbols on a piece of bark while the Plains Indians used hides. Can you etch some symbols on a piece of bark or soft wood?

2. Try writing a story to a friend. This can be a secret coded message. See how close your message can be translated to its actual meaning.

3. The Indians also had a set of number symbols. Try a few math problems.

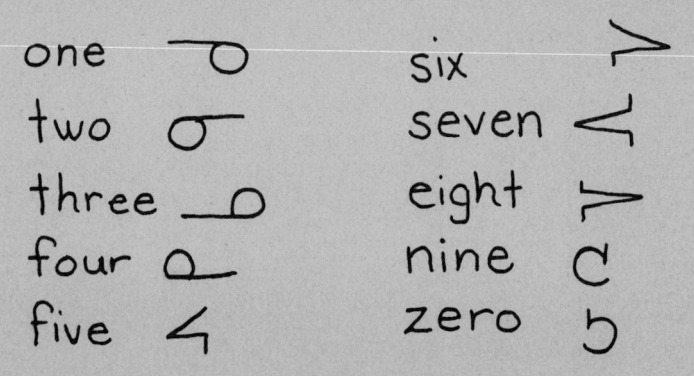

OWNER STICK

History: The Crow Indians of Montana used owner sticks to mark their personal belongings. The stick was about two feet long and had a cross bar near the top. An Indian would decorate the stick so that it was symbolic of his own name. If he had to leave a buffalo skin pegged to the ground to dry and go back to camp, he would put his owner stick in the ground beside it and it would be perfectly safe. Every Indian would honor it.

Procedure: Use a straight, *sturdy stick* twenty four inches long and another *stick* eight inches long for the cross bar. The cross bar may be lashed to the longer stick as shown in Illustration number 1. Use *leather thongs* or *heavy jute string*.

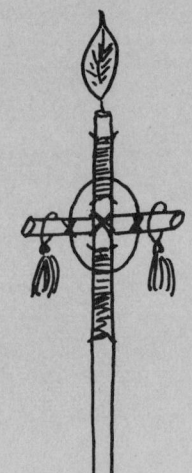

With this basic structure you may use many variations. Bend a piece of *reed* used in basket-making into a circle and attach it to the cross bar. (Illustration number 2.)

You may tie a bunch of *horsehair* or *raveled jute* to the end of the cross bar. (Illustration number 3.)

Using a *drill,* make a small hole in the top of the upright stick and dip a *short feather* in *white glue* to keep it in the hole.

(1)

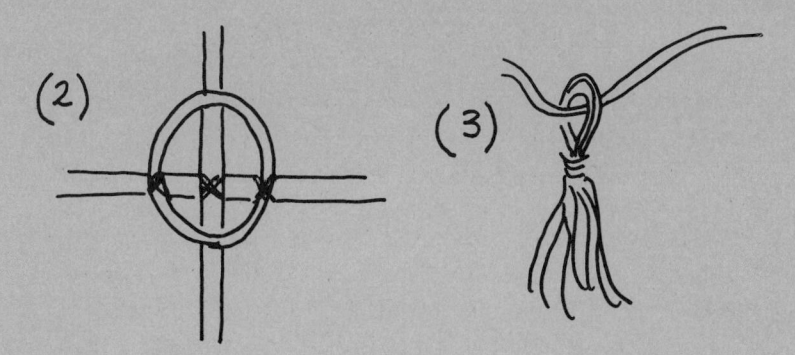

Using shoe *leather* or *cardboard* make a symbol such as an eagle to attach at the cross bar with a leather thong or piece of jute. (Illustration number 4.)

Related Activities:
1. How do we keep our things today when we are away from them? Would the Indian way work?

2. Think of a symbolic name for yourself and use it when making your owner stick. (See Signs and Symbols in this chapter.)

3. Use your owner stick to identify your team meeting place or your cabin at camp. Use it for marking your toss in distance throwing.

INDIAN RATTLES

History: A tribe of Indians living near the Gila River (south of Tucson, Arizona) used rattles with their songs to bring rain. They were also used in treating the sick. Since this tribe lived in the Southwest, they used the natural materials of the desert, such as beans, to make their rattles. The Papago word for "bean" is "papah."

Procedure: Use a *firm stick* about six inches in length and about one half inch in diameter. Indian designs may be etched on the stick. Use a *small brown paper bag* and blow this up with air. Put *six or seven small white beans* into the sack. Now attach the sack to the stick with *masking tape,* making sure no openings are left. The sack may be decorated with Indian signs and symbols relating a story of tribal history. *Feathers* may be attached by tying *twine* around the "neck" of the rattle and tying feathers to each end of the twine. Look for natural materials from your part of the country to decorate the rattles. For example, use *walnut shells,* pretty *rocks, twigs,* and brightly colored *leaves.*

Related Activities:
1. Can you make a rhythm all your own? Try your rattles with some actual Indian music. (See Helpful Books at end of this chapter.)

2. Try different objects inside the rattle. Do larger objects make a different sound? What about smaller objects? Other musical instruments could be made.

For example:
   a. Indian drums
   b. Notched sticks that rub together

c. Small pieces of willow that are tied at one end. When they hit upon your hand they give a whirring sound.

THE BOWL GAME

History: This game was played by Indian tribes throughout the country. In the Southwest a woven basket was used rather than the wooden bowl used by the Woodland and Plains Indians. The winning players would be given anything from arrowheads to ponies by the losers which kept the game exciting.

Procedure: Wash and dry six *plum pits*. Then make a line on one side of each with a *felt tip pen* and put them in a small *bowl*. Holding the bowl in one hand, toss the pits lightly and catch them again in the bowl. Count the number of pits with the lines up. This is your score which you can keep by setting in front of you the correct numbers of *counting sticks,* about *twelve toothpicks* or *twigs* for each player. Have an even number of players sit facing each other on two teams. Pass the bowl to the player directly opposite you for his toss. Continue passing the bowl back and forth remembering that each time a player starts to toss the pits they should be placed marked side down in the bowl. Each player should have at least two turns. Add individual scores together for each team. The winning team has the highest number. Figure out the difference between the two scores. If you wish to play for *gumdrops,* for instance, the losing team gives each member of the winning team the same number of gumdrops as the difference between the scores.

Related Activities:
1. Weave a simple basket or carve a soft pine bowl for the game.

SAND PAINTING

History: Sand paintings are traditionally made by Navajo medicine men. Symbolic designs are formed on the dirt floor of a hogan using crushed red sandstone, charcoal, and colored sand. The design must be started and finished between sun-up and sun-down. By sitting on the design a patient hopes to absorb its power and be cured by the spirits. The intricate sand paintings are swept away by the wind after their use.

Procedure: To make a sand painting that will not be swept away, we can use *white glue* and *cardboard*. The first step is to plan a very simple design. (See Signs and Symbols.) Draw it in lightly with a *pencil* on your cardboard and mark each part with the color you wish to use.

Divide *fine sand* into five *pint containers*. Stir red, yellow, blue, or green *food coloring* into each of the first four containers and leave the sand in the fifth one a natural color. Spread *white glue* evenly into each of the spaces marked blue. Then pour the sand with your fingers over the glue. Pour off the excess into the blue sand container. Do the same with each of the other colors in your design. Each time the sand will stick only to the parts that are covered with glue.

Related Activities:

1. Tell a story about your picture, reading the symbols as if they were words.

2. Name some patriotic symbols of the United States. (See Independence Day in the Holidays chapter.) What does the United States eagle stand for? Is there symbolism in the United States flag? What about your state flag?

3. Find out about the part of the country where the Navajos live and how that determines the kind of life they lead.

CLAY AND KILNS

History of Clay: The nomadic Indians very seldom made pottery as it was too hard to transport. They usually had baskets of all shapes and sizes that would fit closely together and store easily. Clay food bowls were wide and shallow. Cooking pots made by the Papago often had a flat edge for a handle. The Iroquois used a pointed bowl that would fit down in the coals. Undecorated pots were used in the fire and decorated ones were used to eat from and carry water.

Procedure—Making the Clay: Did you know that there is clay in your own back yard? Here is a recipe for making your own earthenware clay.

Using a *shovel,* dig a hole. Usually you can find a clay layer one or two feet down. You can recognize it by its reddish-brown color and its hard-packed texture. Break up the clay and let the sun dry it. Sift it through a *window screen* placed over a *box* or through a smaller *wire strainer* held over a box.

Now put the dried clay (It looks like coffee grounds.) in a *container* and add *water* until it is a soupy mud. Add two tablespoons of *beer* or *milk* for each gallon of liquid and leave it for two weeks. The bacteria break down the tiny chunks and make it easy to mold. Now siphon off the excess water on top with a *cup* or *turkey baster*. Knead the wet clay on *plaster* or *cement* to get rid of the extra moisture. Cover the container.

Procedure—Forming the Clay:

Coil Method: Make a small pancake shape from your clay about the size you want your finished base. Score the outer edge of the base where the coil will be laid. Cover the outer edge of the base with *slip*. Slip is a water and clay mixture that acts as paste. Now take a small piece of clay in your hand and knead it for a few moments. Roll the piece of clay in a rounded strip.

Score the under side and place it on top of the outer edge of the base. Then roll another strip and lay it on top of the first coil. Press it together and smooth all the edges. Add more coils in the same manner. Make the coils into a smooth wall with your fingers, rubbing patiently and slowly. Lay a piece of *cleaning bag plastic* on the top of the bowl to keep the top edge from drying more quickly than the bottom. Uneven drying causes cracks. Let it dry until bone dry. (This is usually about two weeks.)

Pinch Method: Make a ball out of a piece of *clay*. Set the clay ball on a piece of *cleaning bag plastic*. Insert the thumbs of both hands into the middle of the clay ball. Squeeze gently and pull upward using your thumbs on the inside and first two fingers on the outside while turning the bowl constantly. Being slow and careful helps keep the walls uniformly even. If the walls become too thin and flare out, take tucks in the top much as you would in sewing. Fold down the top edge slightly to make it thicker. Then smooth out the tucks in the top edge. You may wish to add handles or lids. Score the ends of the handle pieces as well as the place on the pot where the handles are to be attached. Add slip to both parts and smooth.

History of a Kiln: After setting their pottery on a rack, the Pueblo Indians built a fire around it using for fuel, cedar bark and kindling sticks covered with dry pieces of manure. After the fire had burned to ashes, the pottery was lifted out with long sticks and put on the ground to cool.

Procedure: You can make a primitive kiln in another way by using materials which are readily available.

Lay a floor of *bricks* or *cinder blocks* set close together. Build the walls on top of the floor using more bricks and keeping a slight space (one-half inch) between most of the bricks so that the kiln can get air. If it is windy, use less space; if it is calm, use more. No mortar is necessary.

Place about five inches of fairly *fine, dry sawdust* on the bottom as a bed for the first layer of clay objects. Place the bone dry clay pieces three inches away from the walls and two inches from each other with the heaviest pieces on the bottom. Cover this layer with three more inches of sawdust. Place the clay pieces on top, add another layer if needed and put six inches of sawdust on the top. You may build the walls as you load the kiln.

Place crumpled *newspapers* covered with *dried twigs* on top of the sawdust and light it. Cover with a *metal sheet* and set on *chips of bricks* so that the fire can breathe.

The sawdust should burn slowly and evenly from top to bottom. As it burns it turns black and has occasional sparks, but there should be no flames once it is started. It will take from six to thirty-six hours to burn. Check it occasionally to make sure the fire has not gone out. Re-light if necessary.

The clay varies from being all black to streaked with grays. A pot fired in this manner will not hold water nor can it be eaten from, but children can learn from first hand experience how to build their own kiln rather than relying on one using gas or electricity as its source of energy.

Related Activities:
1. Impressions could be made in the pots with fingernails, pinecones, rocks, and twigs and this will give your pot its own personality.
2. You may make beads for macramé or jewelry by sticking a straw through a small clay shape.
3. Indian pendants could be made with signs and symbols etched into the clay before firing.

INDIAN TRAIL SIGNS

History: The American Indians developed many ways for leaving messages for others to follow. The pioneers and trappers copied their ideas and soon learned their careful technique. The Woodland Indians etched marks in the bark of trees which served as a map for followers. (This should not be done today on public trails.) Other tribes twisted blades of grass or made rock signs. This is an excellent way to make a trail for others to follow.

Procedure: Here is a code for piling rocks to mark a trail.

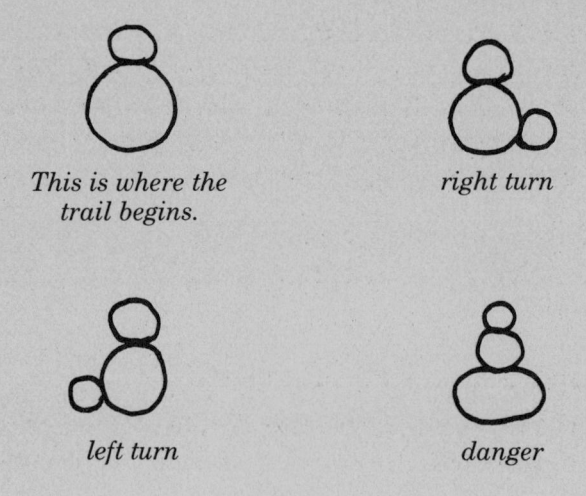

This is where the trail begins.

right turn

left turn

danger

Grasses can be twisted for the same effect.

Trail begins here

right turn

40

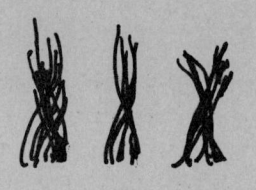

left turn *danger or warning*

Put the signs close together at first so children can become accustomed to them. They will soon discover the fun of searching for these small signals.

Related Activities:
1. Could sticks be laid in a certain way to make a trail? Work with a small group to set up the signals and then have a followup group check to see if they can use the signs and find their way to a designated area. Plan an Indian picnic at the end of the trail.

2. Why would the Indians want to mark a danger area? What other symbols could be used to indicate danger?

Helpful Books for Indian Crafts

Songs and Stories of the North American Indians, Paul Glass, Grosset and Dunlap, New York, 1968.

Indian Crafts, Janet and Alex D'Amato, The Lion Press Publishers, New York, 1968.

Indian Picture Writing, Robert Hofsinde, William Morrow and Company, New York, 1959.

The Indians Secret World, Robert Hofsinde, William Morrow and Company, New York, 1956.

Indian Sign Language, Robert Hofsinde, William Morrow and Company, New York, 1955.

838 Ways to Amuse a Child, June Johnson, Gramercy Publishing Co., New York, 1968.

Indian Arts, Robert Hofsinde, William Morrow and Co., New York, 1971.

Elin's Amerika, Marguerite DeAngeli, Doubleday Doran and Co., Garden City, New York, 1941.

Finding One's Way With Clay, Paulus Berensohn, Simon and Schuster, 1972.

Annie and the Old One, Miske Miles, Little Publishing Co., 1971.

When Clay Sings, Byrd Baylor, Schribner and Sons, 1972.

Helpful Records

Dances and Songs of American Indians, Request Records, Publishers number RLP6028.

Indian Music of the Pacific Northwest Coast, Folkway Records, Publishers number FE4523.

Pioneer Cooking

© 1975 Grayson Slaughter

FUNNEL CAKE

History: Since many of the early settlers of America had to cook on the open fire, cakes were made without the convenience of a bake oven. One such cake was known to the Pennsylvania Dutch as a "Funnel Cake." Its name comes from the utensil that is used to make it, a tin funnel.

Procedure: Beat 1 *egg* in a medium sized *mixing bowl*. Add ⅔ *cup milk*. Sift 1⅓ *cups white flour*, 2 *tablespoons white sugar*, ¼ *teaspoon salt*, ¾ *teaspoon baking powder* and 1 *teaspoon baking soda* together. Add this to the milk and egg mixture and stir until all lumps are dissolved. Fill an *iron skillet* with two inches of *corn oil* or *lard*. Hold your finger over the small end of a ⅜ *inch funnel*. Pour the batter into the large end. Now, remove your finger and, holding the small end of the funnel two inches above the hot oil, drop the batter into the oil in a swirling motion, beginning in the center and working to about eight inches in diameter. The finished cake has the appearance of a child's circular scribble. The batter will puff up. Fry on each side about one and a half minutes using *tongs* to flip. Drain, and sprinkle with powdered sugar. Eat it while it is still hot. The above recipe makes enough for six to eight cakes.

Related Activities:
1. Can you think of other recipes that could be cooked in a skillet in this same way? What about apple fritters? See Johnny Cakes in this chapter.

2. No matter how hard you try, no two funnel cakes will come out the same; however, the Pennsylvania Dutch were also famous for their cast-iron molded candy in which every colorful piece looked exactly like the next. An excellent reference for this molded candy

is *American Cooking—The Eastern Heartland,* by José Wilson. Many types of foods are still made today using molds. Think of as many as you can from your own kitchen and find out about some old fashioned ones.

MAHALA'S APPLE DUMPLINGS

History: The early English settlers brought the idea of meat pies with them but it wasn't until the early immigrants had to use the fruit around them that they developed an apple dumpling, which was very much like an individual apple pie.

Procedure: The following recipe makes enough crust for twelve medium apples. Combine these ingredients with your hands:

- 3 cups unsifted flour
- 1 teaspoon salt
- 1 tablespoon sugar
- 6 tablespoons white shortening
- ½ cup ice water (a little at a time)

Work the dough by squeezing. It should not stick to the dish. (If it does stick you have added too much water.) Flour a piece of *waxed paper* and a *rolling pin*. Roll the dough out thin and cut in five inch strips. Peel and core apples. Lay apples on a five inch square of dough. Combine 12 *tablespoons sugar* and 1 *teaspoon cinnamon* (enough to tint the sugar). Now put one tablespoon of this mixture on each apple. Put 1 *teaspoon butter* on each apple. Pull up the dough and pinch the folds together. Place the twelve dumplings in a buttered *baking dish*. Make sure there is about one inch between each dumpling. Heat the oven to 350 degrees. Put the dumplings on the bottom shelf for the first forty-five minutes and then on the top rack for about ten minutes to brown.

Make a caramel sauce by combining 1 *cup white sugar,* 2 *cups brown sugar* and 4 *tablespoons corn starch.* Add 2 *cups hot water* and cook over moderate heat stirring with a slotted spoon so no lumps will appear. Now stir in 2 *tablespoons butter* and 1 *teaspoon vanilla.* This makes a wonderful sauce for ice cream, cake, or puddings as well as your dumplings.

Related Activities:
1. What else could be put in a dumpling? How would meat and vegetables taste?

2. You could make your own butter as one of the needed ingredients. Here is a quick method. Fill a babyfood jar half full of heavy whipping cream. Shake rapidly until a lump forms. Pour off the butter milk. (How does it taste?) Salt and wash the butter. Set aside to cool.

3. See "Apple Day" in the Holiday chapter for other good apple ideas.

SALT WATER TAFFY

History: Candy making has been a child activity for years. Fondest memories of childhood contain a happy family around a pot of good smelling, bubbling sugars and spices. Sugar and candy making was such a rare treat that it was often an occasion for a whole party of friends and relatives, hence the name "a taffy pull" originated. *Salt* water taffy got its name since it was supposed to be made with sea water. It is still sold along the board-walk of Atlanta, Georgia.

Procedure: Start by mixing 1 *cup white sugar* and 1 *tablespoon corn starch* in a *sauce pan*. Now add ⅔ *cup white corn syrup*, 1 *tablespoon butter* and ½ *cup water*. Cook over moderate heat until a *candy thermometer* shows 254 degrees. If you don't have a candy thermometer you can test by putting a few drops in a dish of cold water and the mixture will form a ball and hold its own shape when it is at the correct temperature. Remove from heat and add *food coloring* and *flavorings* if you wish. Pour the mixture on a *buttered platter*. Cool it until you can handle it easily. Be sure to butter your hands before you start to pull the taffy. Pull it until it becomes light in color. Then pull into a roll, snip off bites and wrap in individual pieces of wax paper.

Related Activities:
1. Plan your own taffy pull. Invite another group to join yours. Can you find some related social customs that went along with a taffy pull? (What other games did they play? What else did they eat? What was the furniture in the home like? What were their clothes like?)

2. Try an experiment—Take the candy off the heat source at a higher or lower temperature. How does the degree of heat affect the texture of candy?

JOHNNY CAKES

History: The Journey Cake or "Johnny Cake" as it came to be called is an old recipe for cornmeal cake. In their travels by wagon train to settle new lands, or when off on wars or hunts, it sometimes happened that pioneers would cook these cakes in a shovel over a campfire.

Cooks had fun exchanging recipes and putting them in rhyme:

> 2 cups Indian, one cup wheat
> 1 cup sour milk, one cup sweet
> 1 cup good eggs that you can eat,
> ½ cup molasses, too,
> ½ cup sugar, add thereto,
>   Salt and soda each a spoon,
>   Mix up quickly and bake it soon.

Procedure: If this seems hard to follow, try this recipe. Mix a *quart of milk,* 3 *eggs,* 1 *teaspoon bicarbonate of soda,* and ⅔ *cup of wheat flour* together. Add Indian *corn meal* until you have a batter like that of pancakes. Bake on a griddle and eat with butter and molasses.

Related Activities:
1. Read the book *Journey Cake, Ho!* by Ruth Sawyer telling how a Johnny Cake got its name. The illustrations tell much about the division of work on a farm.

2. Follow the story of corn from the stalk to your table finding out where it is stored, how it is transported, and how it is made into corn products.

3. Visit a mill (old or new) and learn about the term "wholegrains."

TOASTED PUMPKIN OR SQUASH SEEDS

History: Those settling new lands, such as the colonists and the pioneers as they moved westward, had to be very resourceful to survive. They had to use their imaginations to make use of everything possible in their environment. When crossing the prairies where no trees grew for fuel, children were sent to gather "buffalo chips," or dried manure, for the fires. When mother was making a pumpkin pie, she pickled the rind and saved all of the seeds and toasted them for a family treat.

Procedure: Separate the fiber from unwashed pumpkin or squash seeds. Add to 2 *cups of seeds*, 1½ *tablespoons melted butter or oil* and 1 *teaspoon of salt*. Spread them in a *shallow pan* and bake them in a very slow oven at 250 degrees until they are crisp and brown. Stir them occasionally.

Related Activities:
See "Pumpkin Day" in the Holiday chapter.

CARMEL CORN

History: The first settlers coming to this country from Europe had never before known of corn. They learned of its many uses from the Indians. They devised covered wire baskets with long handles for popping corn kernels over the hot coals.

Procedure: Boil 2 *cups of sugar*, 1 *cup of molasses*, and 2 *tablespoons of vinegar* until the mixture cracks when tested in cold water. You can use a candy thermometer if you would feel safer. After taking it off of the fire, add ½ *teaspoon of baking soda* and beat it well. Pour over *popped corn* and *peanuts* and stir together.

Related Activities:
1. Make your own wire basket for popping corn and try it out.

2. Find out about the history of the company that makes Crackerjack boxes with prizes in the bottom.

3. Find out how sorghum molasses used to be made. It was the main sweetening used by the pioneers.

4. Try making popcorn balls with this recipe by heating the mixture to 250 degrees. Why does the popcorn stick together at this stage?

A MILK CARTON ICE CREAM MACHINE

History: Very primitive versions of ice cream were made over three thousand years ago in China, but it was a purely American version of ice cream that Dolly Madison served at the White House in Washington, D. C. in the early nineteenth century. In the late 1890's it was believed to be a corrupting influence to eat ice cream and soda water on Sunday. Since the operators didn't want to lose sales they mixed ice cream with syrup instead of soda and called it an "Ice Cream Sundae." (The spelling was changed so it wouldn't be confused with the Sabbath.)

Procedure: Mix together in a *large mixing bowl* 3 *eggs* and 1½ *cups white sugar*. Now add ⅛ *teaspoon salt* and 5 *cups milk*. Use 1½ *teaspoons vanilla* for flavoring. Prepare a 1 *gallon milk carton* (cut in half). In the center of the carton put a 6 *oz. metal juice can* and fill it ⅓ to ½ full. Put *ice* in the carton around the can. (Two parts ice to one part *ice cream salt*—found in most grocery stores.) Stir the mixture and move the can in a circular motion until the mixture becomes frozen (about 20-25 minutes). Make sure *no* ice cream salt gets into the juice can mixture. With this method, one ⅓ cup serving can be made at one time. The above ingredients make enough for 12-18 individual servings.

Related Projects:
1. Could you change the flavor of the ice cream by adding fruit?

2. Plantations often had ice houses and the slaves went to great lengths to provide ice for their masters summer drinks. Where did they get the ice? How did they keep it cool during the hot summer months?

JENNIFER'S GINGERBREAD MIX

History: Ginger was a popular spice of the early settlers. The first ginger in America came from England and was later imported from the West Indies. Children young and old delight in its spicy flavor. Ginger tea is an old home remedy for the common stomach ache.

Procedure: Several different recipes can be made from a single Gingerbread mix. Combine all of the following ingredients with two knives until it looks like fine crumbs. Store in a jar in the refrigerator until you are ready to use it.

    8   cups white flour
    2½ cups sugar
    2½ teaspoons baking soda
    2   tablespoons baking powder
    3   tablespoons ginger
    3   tablespoons cinnamon
    1   teaspoon cloves
    1   tablespoon salt
    2½ cups shortening

Use this mix in the following recipes.

Gingerbread Cake

Put 2 cups of the *Gingerbread mix* in a *large mixing bowl*. In another *bowl* combine 1 *egg*, ½ *cup molasses*, and ½ *cup boiling water*. Add this mixture to the dry mixture and stir until all ingredients are smooth. Pour into a greased and floured *pan*. (8 by 8 by 2). Bake at 350 degrees for 35 minutes.

Apple-Gingerbread Pancakes
Original Recipe of the Pioneer Cooking Class—
Wornall House 1975

Combine 1 *cup of the original mix* with ¼ *cup molasses*, ⅓ *cup milk* and 1 *egg*. Add ½ *cup of cooked apple slices*. Stir only enough to moisten. Bake on a *greased griddle*. Serve with *butter* and *powdered sugar*.

Related Activities:
1. To make Gingerbread cookies see the Christmas section in the Holiday chapter.

2. What can you find out about spices in America. Which spices were native to America? Which ones had to be imported? Why did the pioneers treasure their spices?

PEACH LEATHER (Peach Paper)

History: In the fall months of August through October preparations were made for winter. The pioneers made their own butter, cheese, pickles, relish, and jellies. They also cured their own meat and dried the fruit from their orchards. Once in awhile the children made something to satisfy their "sweet tooth."

Procedure: Put 2 *pounds of dried apricots* and 1 *lb. of dried peaches* through a food chopper twice. Dust a small board with *powdered sugar*. Take a small ball of the fruit mixture and roll this out with a *rolling pin* that has been powdered with sugar also. Roll the mixture until it is ⅛ inch thick, and cut into strips. Roll the strips into tight rolls and wrap with wax paper.

Related Projects:
1. What are other ways the pioneers prepared fresh fruit to make it last through the winter months?

2. Discuss the differences between present day and yesteryear ways of food preservation. How was meat preserved all winter? What is beef jerky?

Helpful Books for Pioneer Cooking

The American Heritage Cook Book, American Heritage Magazine, Heritage Press, New York, 1964.

Pioneer Cook Book, Ruth Stone, Theodore Bird Printing, Topeka, Kansas, 1969.

Joy of Cooking, Irma S. Rombauer and Marion Rombauer Becker, Bobbs-Merrill Company, Inc.

Farmer Boy, Laura Ingalls Wilder, Harper and Row, New York, 1941.

Red Flannel Hash and Shoe-Fly Pie, Lila Perl, World Publishers, 1965.

The Naturalist, Down to Earth, Janet Clark, Mary Alice Collins, and Gary Collins, Press Publishing Co., Provo, Utah, 1973.

Sewing, Weaving and Dyeing

EMBROIDERY

History: In George Washington's time, girls rarely went to school. Instead, they learned the art of stitchery, sometimes as early as three years old. Every hand-made stitch is embroidery. Our ancestors brought these beautiful stitches with them across the ocean. The early makers of crazy quilts often signed their names in a delicate embroidery stitch.

Procedure: There are over 300 known embroidery stitches. Here are six easy stitches to get you started. Use a *large-eyed needle* and *embroidery thread* (six strand cotton floss). Strands can easily be separated if necessary for a more delicate stitch. Other stitching could be tried with worsted yarn, silk or linen thread, frayed burlap strands, and kite string.

BACK STITCH

This is a continuous line of small stitches on the right side, and long overlapping stitches on the wrong side.

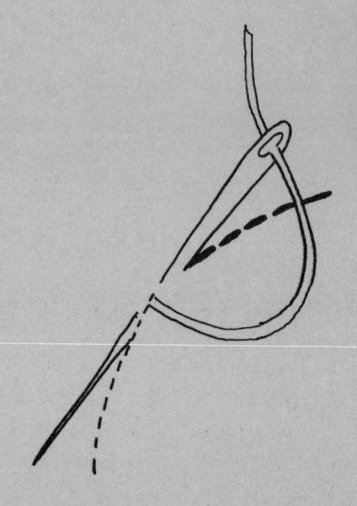

BLANKET STITCH

Work from left to right and hold the thread down with the left thumb.

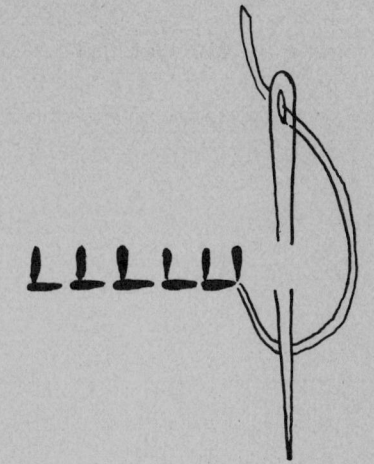

OUTLINE STITCH

Keep thread above needle and bring the needle out a short distance to the left at a slight angle.

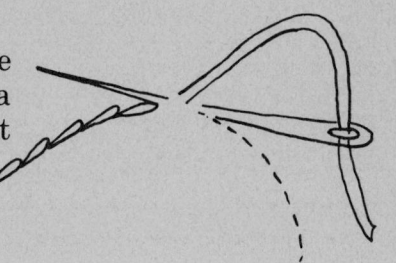

SATIN STITCH

Carry thread underneath fabric. Bring needle up through it again close to beginning of first stitch. Edges must be neat.

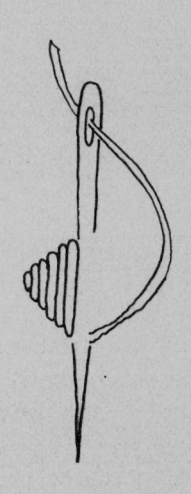

FRENCH KNOT

Bring needle up through fabric where the knot is to be made. Coil thread around needle 2 or 3 times. Insert needle back in fabric close to where it comes out. Pull thread under and secure knot.

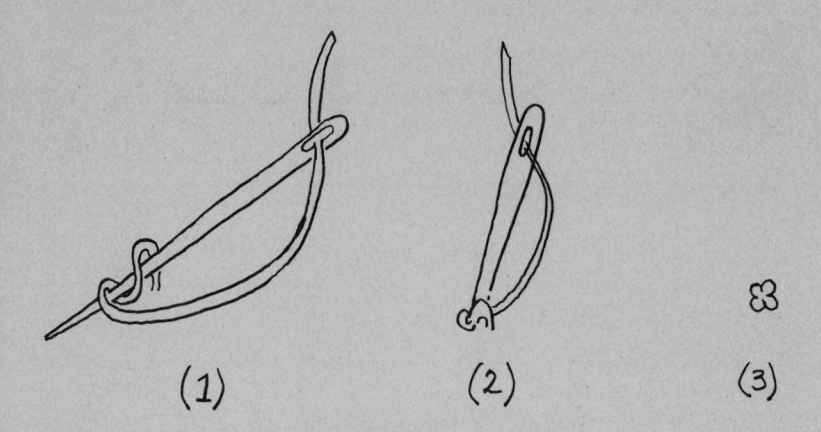

(1)   (2)   (3)

HERRINGBONE STITCH

Bring needle up on left side of lower line and insert a little to the right on upper line. Now do the same on lower line going in the opposite direction.

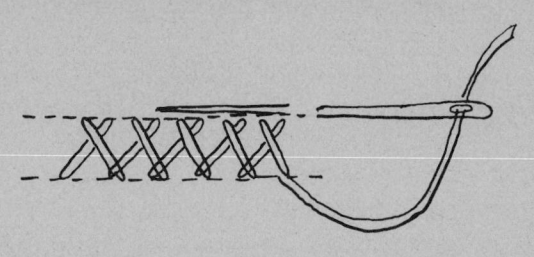

Related Projects:
1. Decorate your own hand towel by making a design and transferring it with dressmakers' tracing paper to fabric. Try decorating a pillow case in the same way.

2. Each child in a classroom could design and decorate his own square. It could then be attached to other classmates squares with a blanket stitch. This wall hanging could represent an era of local or national history. Maybe your finished wall hanging could be a gift to your school or group. Plan a ceremony of presentation.

4. Find out more about Crazy Quilts. They often had intricate embroidery in the odd shaped pieces. This had special meaning for the person making it, or the person receiving the quilt.

APPLIQUÉ

History: In order to use every last scrap of material, pioneer mothers would use appliqué to turn their scraps into pictures. Many of the first quilts in America used an appliqué for the central design. Appliqué is a good exercise in combining patterns, shapes, colors and textures.

Procedure: Make your pattern on thin *tracing paper*. Cut your piece one-fourth inch larger so that you will have enough material to turn under. No raw edges should be visible. Trace around your pattern on a chosen *fabric* with *chalk* or a *pencil*. Whenever possible cut all the pieces to be appliquéd so that the grain runs the same as the background fabric. This will help prevent puckering. Now you are ready to sew the appliqué to the background fabric. Arrange the pieces as you want for the design and hand pin and baste the pieces in place, turning the raw edges under as you go. When all pieces are basted to the background fabric you may do a decorative stitch around all the edges. The most widely used is the blanket stitch which is shown under "Embroidery" in this section. Other embroidery stitches may be added for detail. Press and remove basting.

Related Activities:
1. To achieve a 3-dimensional effect, some antique quilts had cotton batting stuffed between the appliqué piece and the quilt back. Try making the skirt and the bonnet puffy on "Sunbonnet Sue" by adding polyester or cotton batting.

2. Try making an appliquéd "country life" scene. Each item in the scene could be a different fabric pattern.

3. Use your imagination and try a pillow, an apron, a patch, a pocket, a gift for a friend.

PATCHWORK

History: Patchwork quilts were commonplace with pioneer women who stitched scraps of used clothes together to make warm bed covers. The early quilts were filled with dried corn husks and soft grasses or pine needles. Since the life of a colonial woman was very busy, the first quilts were not held together with beautiful stitchery, but rather were tied randomly with twine or yarn. Generations ago American girls were expected to have completed a number of quilts before marrying.

Procedure: Quilts are made in blocks so that once you know how to make one block, you may add more and more to make any size quilt you wish. A four inch square is easy to work with. However, the pattern should measure four and one-half inches on all four sides to allow for seams. Triangles, hexagons, or diamonds can be used, also. The four-patch quilt is a design made up of four squares of two contrasting fabrics.

Press all of the material you will use. A pattern square can be made from *construction paper* or *light-weight cardboard*. Lay the pattern down and trace with a *pencil* or *chalk*. The pattern needs to follow the grain of the *fabric*. Use very *sharp scissors* as cutting is one of the most important steps. When all of the patches are cut, lay them out as you would like the finished project to look. You might want to lay dark and light together or perhaps two solids and two prints in a four-patch square.

If piecing by hand, use a running stitch, and back stitch several times at the ends so the threads will not pull. Simply place the right sides together and stitch one-half inch from the cut edge. Make sure that all of the seams are uniform. Press the seams open flat before joining the other pieces.

Related Activities:
1. Here are some variations to the simple four-patch block.

Use squared paper to draw your own repetitive design and then color it in.

2. Some quilt patterns have unusual names, for instance, Turkey Tracks, Hole in the Barn, Philadelphia Pavements, and Bluebird for Happiness. Find out where these patterns got their names and what they look like.

3. Quilting was popular long before women were allowed to vote. Some of their political preferences were brought out in their quilt names. Here are a few: Lincoln's Platform, Jackson Star, and Democratic Rose. Look in a quilt book to find other ways in which everyday life was shown in quilt designs.

4. Try making a quilt design by using a compass. The circle needs to fit into a square. Could the circle be divided into equal sections?

WOOL

History of Carding: After a sheep is sheared, the raw wool is washed just enough so that it is clean but does not lose its oil, or lanolin, which must be present to spin it. Carding, or combing the wool, separates the fibers which can be formed into fluffy rolls for spinning. Two flat wooden "cards" with handles and tiny bristles are used to pull the wool backwards and forwards between them.

Procedure: Finding and Carding Wool
It is an enlightening experience for children to see and work with raw wool, and worth the effort to find it either locally or by mail order. (Raw wool may be obtained from a 4-H Club; carded rolls from Museum Gift Shop, Old Sturbridge Village, Sturbridge, Mass. 01566; and lamb's wool from a drug store.) A pair of cards can be ordered if none are available to you from E. B. Frye & Sons, Inc., Wilton, N. H. 03086. *Foxfire 2,* edited by Eliot Wigginton, has excellent directions and photographs on carding as well as spinning.

History of Spinning: Man probably first spun with his fingers. Hand and thigh spinning is still practiced by some groups including the Navajos. When spinning with the hands alone, the drawing, twisting, and winding all have to be done separately and it is very slow. Someone discovered that even a hooked stick made spinning easier and eventually many kinds of hand spindles were made. Most colonial homes had a machine called a spinning wheel, invented in the fourteenth century. A "spinster" would sit alongside of it and turn the wheel with a foot treadle while feeding in the fluffy wool.

Procedure: Drop Spindle
A simple method of making a drop spindle uses a *pencil* stuck into the center of a small *apple*.

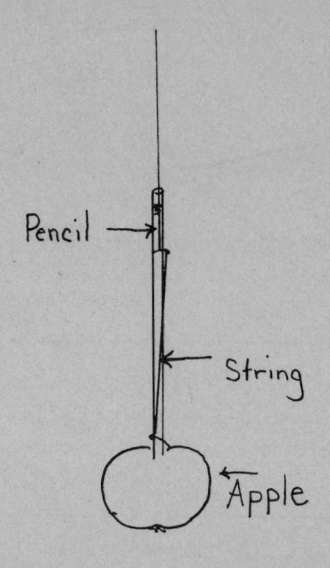

Pencil

String

Apple

Attach a piece of *yarn* by a tight knot or *tape* just above the apple and make a notch in the pencil an inch from the top. Tie the yarn with a half hitch loop around the notch and fray the end which is about four inches in length. Hold the short end of the spun yarn in the left hand as well as the carded roll of wool to be spun. Lay the spun end at the beginning of the roll and holding on to both, twirl the spindle with your right hand. The twisting motion and the weight of the whorl (the apple in this case) will combine the two pieces of wool into one. Keep attaching more rolls in the same way.

History: Dyeing
Primitive man used colors to ward off evil spirits. Soon colored symbols were made and art was born. The first dyes were probably stains from berries and fruits.

There is some effort in using dyes, but the beauty and rich colors that come from nature make it worth it.

Mordants are used to help make the dye a part of the wool and to keep it from fading. Some mordants found in the kitchen are alum, salt, vinegar, and cream of tartar. There are some dyes that are strong enough by themselves and do not need a mordant, such as mulberries, onion skins, and walnut hulls. Use a mordant with most other dyes.

Procedure: Dyeing
If you want to mordant your material or yarn before dyeing, the following is an example of the proportions you need:

> 2 Tablespoons cream of tartar or alum
> in each gallon of water
> for every pound of fabric or yarn.

You will need a container. The type you choose effects the colors.

> Copper—light, bright colors
> Iron—dark colors
> Enamel, stoneware, ceramic pots—generally add a mordant
> Stainless steel—may be used but the pot may become stained.
> Aluminum—*never* use for dyeing.

Gather the *plant material* and chop it up or crush it. As an example of proportions, use two cups of papery onion skins to twelve cups of water. Then simmer it for fifteen minutes to two hours depending on the intensity of the color that you want. After cooling it and straining out the plant material, you are ready to dye. Stir the yarn gently with a wooden utensil to avoid tangles. Squeeze out and drip dry in the shade. If your yarn does not dye evenly, it means that your container is too small. The following is a list of plants and the colors that you may expect to get from them.

> yellow—marigold blossoms, yellow onion skins (alum)
> brown—coffee, tea, walnut hulls
> blue—sunflower seeds, blueberries
> green—spinach leaves
> red—raspberries, cranberries, red onion skins
> purple—purple petunia blossoms (cream of tartar)

History: Weaving
By the time the colonists came to the New World, man had probably been weaving six thousand years already. So they brought with them centuries of knowledge and some sheep and began spinning and weaving homespun. The British government tried to forbid the colonists to make their own cloth in hopes they would buy expensive English broadcloth, but it made the patriotic Americans even more determined to stand on their own. At Mount Vernon George Washington had a flock of 800 sheep and his staff wove at least a yard of cloth each day. When the industrial revolution came in the nineteenth century, almost all home weaving died out and factories began producing woven goods.

Procedure: Wall Hanging
Make a loom by cutting notches with *scissors* one-half inch apart across the top and bottom of a piece of *heavy cardboard*. The cardboard should measure slightly more on all sides than the desired size of the finished weaving. String the lengthwise *yarn,* called the warp, by winding a piece of yarn on both sides of the cardboard from a notch on the top through the notch on the bottom directly under it and so on. Go

through the first and last notches twice to hold the yarn in place leaving about six inches extra on each end.

The crosswise yarn is called the weft and is woven over one strand of lengthwise yarn and under the next. Since this is a wall hanging, it is not necessary to have a continuous piece of yarn for the weft. An interesting design might use several thicknesses and colors of yarn as well as *natural materials* such as wheat stems, twigs, clover or seed pods. Keep your weaving tight by pushing your rows together as you work. When you have woven all you can on one side of the cardboard, cut the warp yarn across the middle on the back of the loom. Tie each two pieces of yarn together around a *stick* which is used as a bar at the top of the weaving. Cut off the extra ends. Knot the yarn together at the bottom in the same manner, but instead of cutting off the extra yarn, let it hang as fringe or try threading nuts, pebbles or beads on the ends.

Related Activities:
1. Compare cotton fibers and wool fibers under a microscope.

2. Today sheep are sheared by the thousands with electric shears. How was it done before electricity?

3. Have someone experienced in spinning bring a spinning wheel to class and demonstrate its use. Your local historical society, a specialty shop selling hand-spun products, or a university with a fiber department may be of help locating this special person.

4. After reading some of the resource books listed in this chapter, make a list of terms used in talking about wool such as rolag, whorl, and lanolin. A matching card game could be devised by writing the word on one card and the definition on another.

5. Using one kind of plant, make a dye bath in three different types of pots, such as copper, iron, and stoneware. How does the container affect the color? Now try using the same type of pot (either enamel, ceramic or stoneware), the same plant material, and the same type of yarn, but vary the mordant you use in each of three pots. Keep a chart recording the outcome of your combinations. What happens if you put three or four rusty nails in a dye pot?

6. Use some macramé knotting in your weaving to create interesting spaces. You may dye strips of wool cloth to weave across instead of yarn. Try going over two rows and under two rows to see what pattern you can create.

**Helpful Books
(for Embroidery, Appliqué and Patchwork)**

Decorative Stitchery, for Embroidery, Appliqué and Patchwork, Marian May, Lane Books, Menlo Park, Calif., 1971.

PatchWork and Other Quilting, Linda S. Weeks, Sterling Publishing Co. Inc., New York, 1973.

Early American Crafts and Hobbies, Raymond F. and Marguerite Yates, Wilfred Funk, Inc. New York, 1954.

The Romance of the Patch Work Quilt in America, Carrie A. Hall, Rose G. Kisetsinger, Bonanza Books, New York, 1935.

Needlework and Embroidery, Winifred Butler, Castle Books, New York, 1967.

Basic Stitches of Embroidery, Gisela Hein, Van Nostrand Reinhold Co., New York, 1971.

Helpful Books For Wool

Cloth from Fiber to Fabric, by Walter Buehr, Wm. Morrow and Co., N.Y., 1965.

Man is a Weaver, Elizabeth Chesley Baity, Viking Press, N.Y., 1942.

The Weavers, Leonard Everett Fisher, Franklin Watts, Inc., N.Y.

The Story Book of Wool, Maud and Miska Petersham, The John C. Winston Co., Philadelphia.

Foxfire 2, ed. Eliot Wigginton, Anchor Books, N.Y., 1973.

Pelle's New Suit, Elsa Beskow, Horrow Pub. Co., 1929.

Holidays

© 1975 Grayson Slaughter

OLD-FASHIONED VALENTINES

History: Valentines arrived in this country when the Puritans settled in the Massachusetts Bay Colony. They had been a tradition in England since the fifteenth century when men began to write messages of love and send them to their sweethearts. At that time "valentine" meant "sweetheart."

For many years valentines were handmade. By 1823 books called valentine writers were being sold to give unoriginal writers ideas for verses. Here is one:

> The rose is red,
> The violet blue,
> Lillies are fair,
> And so are you.

The Pennsylvania Dutch people were famous for their lacy cutout work, pinprick designs, and bright colors. Because valentines shared very personal thoughts, the sender often enclosed a lock of hair or a silhouette picture of himself so his sweetheart would remember him. There was such a thing as a vinegar valentine, too, that ridiculed the person who received it and was rarely signed.

In the mid nineteenth century Christmas was the only holiday more popular than Valentine's Day. By this time there were factories making the cards and a good postal system to deliver them.

Although traditionally men sent valentines to women, during the Civil War many soldiers received valentines from their sweethearts. Some were window valentines with tent flaps that opened up showing a soldier inside, or paper doll valentines having printed faces and feet and cloth dresses. There was even one called a tussie mussie in which each flower or herb in a picture bouquet had a special meaning.

By the 1880's the valentines became very ornate with cupids, tassels, paper flowers, ribbons, satin centers and lace edges. In the early twentieth century the invention of the automobile brought mechanical valentines with moving wheels.

REBUS VALENTINE

A rebus is a valentine verse that has words represented by pictures or symbols whenever possible. See if you can read this old verse and write some of your own.

👁 would 👁 could
My ♡ convey
2 U my love
in this 💐

WINDOW VALENTINE

Often the "windows" which opened in these valentines were church doors revealing a bride and groom being married. You may want to design a window valentine using your home, a school bus, or even a box of candy with a lid that flips up, as the picture.

Cut a piece of *construction paper* in half and use one of these halves for your *crayon* design. Cut your openings on three sides leaving the fourth as a hinge for opening and closing. *White glue* will hold the second half of the construction paper to the back of the picture. Draw hidden messages and pictures behind the openings.

Like this valentine, the first paper valentines were similar to post cards and did not open up.

LOVE APPLES

Tomatoes were once called love apples and grew in Victorian flower gardens. Instead of being eaten, they were admired for their shiny red beauty. Valentines were sometimes made in the shape of a tomato with a verse inside.

Fold your *paper* and draw a tomato shape with leaves and a stem at the top. Cut it out with *scissors* leaving the fold on the left side. Color in details with *crayons* on the front and write a verse on the inside.

A PAPER HAND

In the nineteenth century a popular token of love was a paper hand. This was chosen as a symbol because during courtship a man would ask for a woman's hand in marriage. Before paper hands were used as cards, real gloves were often given as a valentine gift. Party cookies were cut out with tin cutters in the shape of a hand with a heart in the center.

You can make a card by folding a piece of *construction paper* in half and tracing with *pencil* around your hand. Your wrist should be on the fold. Cut around your lines with *scissors* leaving the fold at the wrist as a hinge. A paper heart in a contrasting color may be attached with *glue* to the glove. Here is an old verse for your "love glove."

> If that from Glove
> You take the G,
> Then glove is Love
> Which I send thee.

THREE-DIMENSIONAL DESIGNS

Valentines became more ornate as the celebration of Valentine's Day became more popular. They were laden with trimmings by 1880.

Here are some suggestions for making this kind of valentine. Cut apart parts of *old cards* or pictures with *scissors* and stick them back together in three-dimensional layers with *glue*. Cut the center out of a paper lace *doily* and use it as a frame which stands out from the card with paper strip springs made by folding the paper in opposite directions several times. The picture in the frame may be of a beautiful girl, a pastoral scene, cupids, hearts and flowers. Tuck in tiny *ribbons,* artificial *flowers* and paper love *doves*. Use *sequins, feathers, glitter* and pieces of old *jewelry* to complete your romantic card.

WINNING WORDS

Valentines have frequently had whimsical verses as well as serious and flowery ones. Here is an example:

> If you were Miss Muffet
> Who sat on a tuffet
> Eating of curds and whey,
> And I were the spider
> Who sat down beside her,
> I never would scare you away.

Try making up a new verse from another old rhyme.

SHE LOVES ME

For centuries children have played this game in many different versions. Here are two ways using apples.

Think of a particular girl and repeat "She loves me,

she loves me not" with every two twists of an apple stem. After twisting several times, the stem will break off. If you were saying "she loves me" when it broke, she *does* love you. Of course, the opposite is true if you were saying "she loves me not."

Girls can think of boys names, too. Save every seed from your apple and arrange them in line repeating this old verse as you touch each seed.

> One I love, two I love
> Three I love, I say.
> Four I love with all my heart,
> Five I cast away.
> Six he loves, seven she loves,
> Eight they both love;
> Nine he comes, ten he tarries,
> Eleven he courts, Twelve he marries.

EASTER

History: The birth of Christ is celebrated at Christmas, while His death and resurrection is celebrated at Easter. Astronomers helped set the date of Easter. They decided that Easter should come on the next full moon after the first day of spring. A full moon was needed for travelers, as many Christians wanted to be with family and friends during this great celebration.

America became a "melting pot" of the world. People brought their ideas and religious customs with them to their new land. Easter has remained a Christian holiday in our country.

Easter Symbols: The pioneer settlers of Fredricksburg, Texas told a very different story about Easter. It seems a German family had seen Indian campfires burning in the distance. The time was Easter Eve and the mother didn't want her children to become alarmed. She told them that the Easter rabbit had started the fires to heat the kettles as he was dyeing Easter eggs. Ever since, the town of Fredricksburg has lighted fires around the area.

Other symbols of Easter have appeared. Where do you think the pioneers got the idea of the Easter lamb? Hot Cross Buns were supposed to be given to the very poor in England. What about Easter lilies? Do they have an interesting story to tell? A research project would be an excellent way to find answers to these and many other questions about our Easter holiday.

Easter Eggs with Natural Dyes: Eggs have been known as a symbol of life for centuries. Some countries forbid the eating of eggs during Lent and then on Easter they became a wonderful delight. In England, priests often blessed eggs which were then eaten. An old German legend says there once lived a poor old woman who loved boys and girls, but she was very sad one Easter because she had no money to buy treats for her young friends. Fortunately though, she did have many eggs which she dyed beautiful colors and hid in her garden in small nests. Just as the children found the eggs a rabbit hopped out. "Oh," cried the children, "Look what the rabbit has left us!"

The pioneers used natural dyes to carry on their traditions. Eggs can be boiled while they are being dyed. Bring the *dye batch* to a hardy boil. Add the *eggs* and reduce the heat so they will bubble slowly. Add a *teaspoon of vinegar* and enough *water* to cover the eggs. Here is a chart to form your colors.

        light yellow — orange peels
        yellow green — pear peelings
        orange   — onion skins
        brown   — coffee
        blue   — red cabbage
        purple   — cranberries

Try a few experiments with your colors. The Pennsylvania Dutch brought the idea of scratching designs on already colored eggs. Tiny tulips, hearts and flowers were etched with a sharp needle. A delicate touch and a great deal of patience was needed!

An Easter Parade: With Spring comes the feeling of newness that has often been associated with cleaning and happiness. This was often the time when children were given a bath and told they could remove their long winter underwear, and put on lighter weight clothes. Hats were worn to church by many of the townspeople, especially hats with flowers.

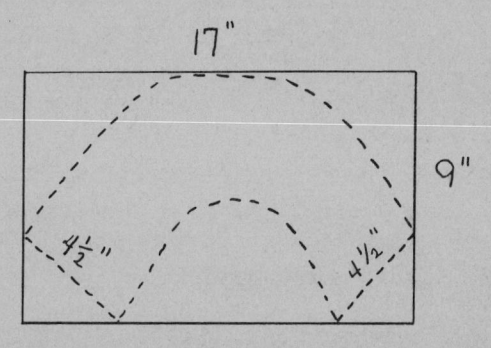

Hats are always loved by children. Make your own creation special by using *ribbon, lace, yarn* and *paper*

flowers. Here is an easy basic pattern for your creation. Cut out the shape from *construction paper* and staple the two ends to fit each child.

Ribbons under the chin may be added to help secure the hat. Now you are ready for your Easter parade. Use a tape recorder to interview the models having them each describe their own creation.

Easter Egg Games: Wherever Easter is celebrated there are always egg games and egg contests. On the White House lawn every year, children roll eggs down the sloping green. There are prizes and the President comes for the event.

Children may roll hard cooked eggs down a hill or toss them in the air to see whose can "fly" the highest. Players could take turns rolling eggs to a hole to see whose egg can go in first. There is an old Easter game similar to our Pin the Tail on the Donkey. A large picture of a rabbit is drawn with outstretched paws. Each player is blind-folded and is given an egg. He then tries to pin his egg in the rabbit's paws.

INDEPENDENCE DAY

History: Our proudest holiday represents the beginning of our nation. On July 4th, 1776 the Congress announced the adoption of the Declaration of Independence. Bells called the people to the town square in Philadelphia, Pennsylvania. A crowd gathered and a man read the words of the Declaration written by Thomas Jefferson. The Declaration told the world that America considered itself free from England's rule. The news spread slowly since men traveled by wagon, horseback and boat.

John Adams said that the day Congress signed the

Declaration should always be remembered. Gradually over the years came a pattern of the "old-fashioned Fourth," celebrated in the public squares with cannon salutes at sunrise and sunset, parades of militia units, floats, bands, and a few exciting games. After the parade came the singing of national songs, the reading of the Declaration of Independence, and the highlight, a lengthy patriotic speech.

The western settlers celebrated the occasion when time and resources permitted. Each year, July 4th is set aside as a day to reaffirm our belief and love of our country.

AN INDEPENDENCE DAY PARADE

> Squeek the fife and beat the drum
> Independence Day has come!

Young and old alike love parades. Why not plan one? Start it off with a patriotic speech telling why you are proud of your country. Decorate your *bike* and turn your *wagon* into a float. Find *clothes* that are red, white, and blue and make them into patriotic costumes. George Washington wore a 3 cornered hat during the Revolutionary War. Here is an idea for a *newspaper* parade hat.

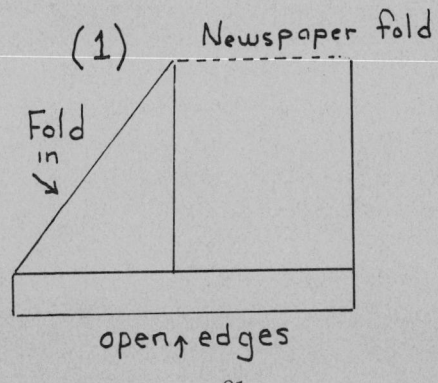

(1) Newspaper fold
Fold in
open edges

(2) Fold in ←

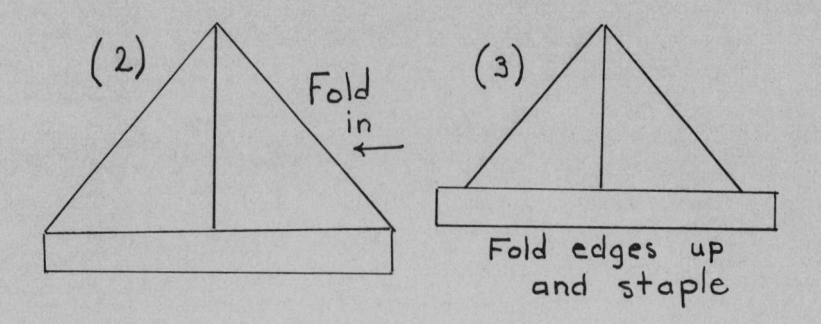

(3) Fold edges up and staple

When you have made your hat, *paint it* and stick a *feather* in it like Yankee Doodle did. Imagine yourself as a drummer boy with a *coffee can drum* or a *pie pan* and *wooden spoon*. Here is a song to sing about your hat! Sing the verse all the way through the first time. The second time you sing the song, touch your head instead of singing the word "hat." The third time, touch your head and hold up three fingers for the word "three." When you sing the song the last time, leave out the word "hat" and "three" and make a sign for the word "corners" with your thumb and first finger.

In 1776, the fife was a popular instrument and it was like many of today's whistles. Find your whistle and give your friend a harmonica.

My Hat

My hat it has three cor-ners   Three corners has my hat
And had it not three cor-ners — It would not be my hat.

Don't leave your pets out of the fun as animals were always included!

FOURTH OF JULY SYMBOLS

In 1898 Spain and America were fighting the Spanish-American War. On July 4, 1898, the day after winning an important naval battle, the Americans blew up the gun powder of the captured Spanish ships. Many other countries had celebrated holidays with firecrackers, but this was probably the first time it had been done in America.

Independence Day is a good time to study other American symbols. Was there a real person known as Uncle Sam? Clues can be found in a study of the War of 1812 or a study of the U. S. Post Office. Where did the Liberty Bell come from? Where did the Washington Monument and the Statue of Liberty come from?

A "COUNTRY FAIR"

The 4th of July is a traditional time for a country fair. Here are some ideas for setting up an old-fashioned fair in your community.

Get your friends together with a good flag book. *(Flags of American History,* by David D. Cruthers) and let each person pick a favorite flag from American history to color on *paper* or *material* for display at the fair.

Some old time fun could include games played by all. A pie-eating contest, a sack race, a watermelon seed spitting contest, pony rides, and a cake walk are easy to organize and fun for others to watch. One old game displays a *picture of the Liberty Bell.* Using *five bean bags* the children get five turns to hit the bell and make it "ring."

Every community has skilled craftsmen such as weavers, wood carvers, and potters who may enjoy doing demonstrations of their crafts and maybe even bring a few crafts to sell.

It may be fun to have several booths where people make old-fashioned toys and games. (See Toys and Dolls.) The aroma of freshly cooked funnel cakes (See Pioneer Cooking) will lure prospective customers.

Because this is a day we reaffirm our belief in our country and express our pride in it, you may want to share your profits with an organization that is making America a better place in which to live.

APPLE DAY

History: Crabapples smaller than golf balls and very bitter were the only apples in this country when the Pilgrims arrived. They planted seeds brought from Europe which produced large, sweet apples. As the pioneers moved west, they planted apple trees along the trails where they settled. One of these people was a wandering preacher, John Chapman, better known as Johnny Appleseed.

ANTIQUE APPLE TOOLS

Plan your apple activities for the fall when apples are hard, juicy, and full of flavor. There are many kinds of old-fashioned kitchen tools used in the preparation of apple dishes such as a corer, a hand-crank peeler, and a six-sectioned slicer and corer combination. Cranking an apple-peeler can set the mood of the country kitchen, can demonstrate the differences in kitchen appliances then and now, and can be fun to use for a "longest peel" contest. A local antique shop may loan you one if none of your friends still use them.

APPLE MAGIC

In every single apple lies
A truly magical surprise.
Instead of slicing down, slice through
And watch the star appear for you.

Margaret Hillart

APPLE PICKING

Plan an apple picking trip to an orchard. Apples cost less when you pick them yourself and children can see first-hand where apples come from.

APPLESAUCE

Wash, peel, core, and quarter twelve *apples*, about three cups. Place in a pot and partly cover them with water. New apples need very little water, old ones need more. Stew until tender for an hour or more. Put them through a *strainer* and season to taste with *sugar* or *lemon*. Sprinkle with *cinnamon*.

P.S. Some cooks do not peel their apples. Applesauce will turn pink when the skins of red apples are stewed (but strained out of the sauce) and more vitamins are retained.

SCHNITZ

"Schnitz" means any variety of dried apples and is a Pennsylvania Dutch word. Many foods were preserved by drying for the long winter months. In colonial times apple rings were dried in several ways. Sometimes they were sliced in rings and hung on strings near the fireplace or from the rafters. At other times apple slices were placed in cooling bake ovens. Large orchards had "dry houses" which were small, windowless buildings heated by stone or brick furnaces. The fruit was placed on slotted wooden trays and stirred often.

Today we can use a modern oven set at 150 degrees. Place the *apples* sliced one-half inch thick in a single layer on a *cookie sheet* lined with *wax paper*. Bake for several hours. The apples should be firm to the touch with no moisture.

Schnitz can be stored in tightly closed paper bags and kept indefinitely in a cool, dry place. Schnitz mixed with raisins would be a scrumptious old-time snack.

APPLE A B C'S
Make a simple book using sheets of construction paper 8½ by 11 inches or 8½ by 5½ inches. Fold these pages in half. Keep the folded pages together by punching two holes on the crease and tying them with yarn on the outside. Your book may have from eight to twenty-six pages depending on how much you want to stretch your imagination thinking up words. Go through the alphabet thinking of an apple activity for each letter such as "A is for apple pie," "B is for bobbing," "C is for cutting." Then using *felt tip pens* or *crayons* illustrate each page.

Kate Greenway wrote and illustrated a book called *A is for Apple Pie*. You may enjoy reading it after you have made your books. Notice the old-time words she uses.

APPLE BOBBING
There is more than one way to catch an *apple* in your mouth. Core an apple with a *knife*. Tie one end of a *string* through the hole and the other end around a tree branch or ceiling beam. Without letting the swinging apple touch anything but your face, you must catch it in your teeth.

In another version a number of apples are floating in a tub of water. You must catch one with your teeth, but it is all right to let the apple touch the side of the tub. Just be sure your hands are behind your back!

APPLE POMANDER

As long ago as the middle ages spiced pomanders were popular with the nobility in England who hung them from belts at their waists. Clove orange apple balls are mentioned in *Little House in the Big Woods* by Laura Ingalls Wilder.

Tie two *ribbons* one-half inch in width and 2½ feet in length around an *apple*. Anchor the two ribbons at the bottom with a *straight pin*. The long ends may be tied around a rod to dry for two weeks in a warm, dry place.

Stick *cloves* all over the unpeeled apple. They do not have to be touching each other because as the apple dries, it shrinks and the cloves draw closer together. Shake it in a bag with about two teaspoons of *cinnamon* and a teaspoon of *orris root*. (This is optional but can be found at herb shops and some drug stores. One ounce is enough for about 10 apples.)

Hang your finished pomander in a closet to give it a pleasant old-fashioned scent.

PRINT APPLE FRACTIONS

Cut an apple in half. A good stamp pad is a *sponge* soaked with *tempera paint*. Press the apple half on the pad and then on a piece of *construction paper*. Cut fourths and eighths of the apple and print with these pieces noticing their relationship in size to the half. Think of ways to use repetition and balance to make your design more pleasing to the eye. Notice the difference in shape when you cut the apple horizontally. Does it make a difference in the size of the fractions?

SPROUT YOUR OWN
Let your apple seeds ripen by putting them on damp paper in a jar, covering them with more damp paper. Put them in the refrigerator. If you keep them moist for six to eight weeks, they will sprout. During the ripening, chemical changes take place in the seeds that help them sprout. Can you find out more about these chemical happenings from books and your observations?

GROWING QUESTIONS
How are new varieties of apples begun? What is grafting? How long does it take for a seed to grow to be a mature tree?

APPLE RIDDLE
How many seeds are there in an apple?
How many apples are there in a seed?

HALLOWEEN AND PUMPKIN DAY

History: By the time the colonists arrived, wild varieties of small and bitter squash and pumpkin had already been replaced by a sweet and fleshy kind cultivated by the Indians. This delicious, nutritious fruit came about almost by accident. Indians cultivated pumpkins for their use as rattles rather than food. As they tended their pumpkin patches over the centuries, the pumpkins became bigger and sweeter.

SAY "HELLO"
Before you carve your pumpkin, feel the difference in texture between the skin and the stem. Why does a pumpkin have ridges? With your eyes closed see if you can smell the pumpkin before you carve it. Can you smell the inside of the pumpkin after it is carved? Does moisture make things have a stronger odor? Think up some experiments to find out what makes things smell.

JACK-O-LANTERNS AND FUNNY FACES

Using a *carving knife,* cut a circle from the top of the *pumpkin.* Pry off the hat and scrape out the seeds and loose fiber with a *large metal spoon.* Save the seeds for experiments and for eating. Design a face with crayon on the pumpkin being careful not to get the mouth too low. Carve away the features. Light a *candle* and hold it horizontally so that hot wax will drip in a puddle inside the pumpkin. Press the bottom of the candle in the melted wax and put the hat back on. Flashlights can be substituted for candles.

You can make pumpkins into funny faces without hollowing them out at all by attaching vegetables to the outside. A long pointed *carrot* may protrude from a small hole cut out with a knife to become a nose. Fat slices of *cucumbers* can become eyes attached with a long *nail.* Halved *radishes* may form a mouth. What would your pumpkin look like with *corn husk* hair and a *corn tassel* mustache?

Another modern day variation might be called a "junk-o-lantern," a pumpkin decorated with castaways such as *light bulbs, springs, packing materials, fabric scraps,* and *cardboard tubes.*

You may have fun having a "Pumpkin Panorama" show where *prizes* are awarded in various categories, for instance, 1. Best all-round pumpkin, 2. Scariest, 3. Most articles added, 4. Most intricate carving, 5. Most creative use of the shape, and 6. Funniest.

PUMPKIN PRINTS

After you have finished your jack-o-lantern, you can use the pieces that you carved away for printing. Using a *paring knife* slice off the inside surface so that it is flat. Make a stamp pad with a thin *sponge* soaked in *poster paint.* Cut colored *burlap* with *scissors* in the shape of a pumpkin and print a face. Of course, you could carve your printing pieces into many other shapes, too.

THE SECRET LIFE OF AN EVERYDAY PUMPKIN

What does your pumpkin do at night when the moon comes out? What happened when your pumpkin had a hormone shot and would not stop growing? How does it feel to be a pumpkin-head scarecrow? How did the moon and the pumpkin become good friends?

Children will enjoy making up stories to answer these questions. It would be fun, too, to make up a question for a friend to answer. Get together in a small group and let everyone add to the story as it develops. Oral creative story-telling can lead to written creative prose or poetry.

PUMPKIN STEM WHISTLE

You may have made a grass blade vibrate in a loud shriek by blowing on it, or made a dandelion-stem pipe. But have you ever tried using a pumpkin stem for a whistle? It makes a deep, rich sound.

PUMPKIN SEEDS

Split open a pumpkin seed with a sharp *paring knife*. Use a *magnifying glass* to look carefully at its contents. What parts do all seeds have in common? Why is a pumpkin classified as a fruit?

Line a glass with wet paper towels and place the seeds of a pumpkin between the glass and the paper. Put one inch of water in the bottom of the glass. Watch for the "root peg" which is the first part of the seed to sprout. This holds apart the two halves of the seed coat while the seed leaves grow out.

PUMPKIN FIGURES

Use a *tape measure* around the broadest part of the pumpkin to discover its diameter. Convert the inches to centimeters.

Weight estimates may be written on a piece of paper placed in front of several pumpkins. Guess the weight and then weigh the pumpkins on *scales* to check your estimate. The number of pounds a five-year-old weighs is often as much as his height in inches. Does this rule apply to pumpkins?

A PUMPKIN COACH

Many of America's holiday traditions were brought here from other countries. When Irish and Scottish settlers came, they celebrated Halloween ("hallowed or holy evening") with parties, decorations and refreshments. A popular decoration was a hollow pumpkin coach filled with candy, apples and raisins pulled by a team of rats and driven by a witch.

To duplicate this for your home or classroom, set your *pumpkin* in a steady position with the stem on top. Using a *long knife* cut away a quarter section of the pumpkin leaving the stem on top. Hollow it using a *large metal spoon* and add *doughnuts* for wheels.

The witch that is perched in the driver's seat can be made from a carved dried *apple* with a *wire* frame body. (See Apple-Head Pop-up Puppet in the Toys and Dolls chapter.) Her flying black dress does not need to be fitted. Try some wild orange hair made from frayed *jute* or *yarn* and a tall *black paper* hat. She will be holding the reins for the team of rats.

In the earliest versions of this decoration the rats were real stuffed rats, but they can be made from a simple paper sculpture technique.

John Greenleaf Whittier wrote about a pumpkin in this following well-known verse.

> Oh, fruit loved of boyhood, the old days recalling,
> When wood-grapes were purpling and brown nuts were falling,
> When wild, ugly faces we carved in its skin,
> Glaring out through the dark with a candle within!
> When we laughed round the corn-heap, with hearts all in tune,
> Our chair a broad pumpkin—our lantern the moon,
> Telling tales of the fairy who travelled like steam,
> In a pumpkin-shell coach, with two rats for her team!

THANKSGIVING AND CORN DAY

History: In many countries throughout the world it has been a custom to give special thanks at harvest time, but the Pilgrims started the American Thanksgiving. In 1620 the Mayflower landed at Cape Cod but finding unfriendly Indians, the Pilgrims resettled at

Plymouth Plantation across the bay. One hundred and two passengers came on the Mayflower, and thirty-two of these were children. Their voyage lasted sixty-six days. The only signs of Indians having been there was cleared ground and some corn. The winter came and over half of the Pilgrims became sick and died. With Spring came a feeling of rebirth and they planted wheat and barley from seed they had brought from England. Friendly Indians showed them how to plant corn, beans, and squash.

At harvest time in October, 1621, the Pilgrims held their first Thanksgiving. Ninety braves brought deer to eat, while the Pilgrims prepared other parts of the meal. Games and contests were played after the feasting.

Each November in America we give thanks to God for our homes, and food and safety in our land, and we remember the struggle of the Pilgrims who gave us our first Thanksgiving.

History of Corn in America: In the Spring of 1621 two friendly Indians appeared. Their names were Samoset and Squanto, and they belonged to the Wampanoag tribe. The Pilgrims and the Indians made a treaty of peace. Squanto taught them to put three fish (herring) in each mound of corn seeds. There is little doubt that the colonists could have survived without corn. It was a sturdy plant and little plowing or clearing was necessary. The corn grew rapidly and the Pilgrims found many uses for it. They watched the Indians braid the husks and make beautiful mats and baskets. Dried corn husks also made a good filler for quilts, and even corn husk dolls appeared. The early celebrations of Thanksgiving were never without corn.

"CORNEY MATH"

Observe an ear of corn. The kernels are always in pairs, so there is always an even number of rows on each cob. The computation of the number of kernels in a row and on the ear can be an interesting lesson for young children. Estimate the number of kernels first. Then, count one row and multiply by the number of rows. How many kernels does a six inch ear of corn have? Is the number an even one or an odd one? Do the kernels disappear in pairs? Can you count by twos to two hundred?

CORN-COB ANIMALS

The Pilgrims learned to use every part of the corn plant. Cobs were even used for cooking fuel. The children soon found a use for unused cobs and made corn cob toys. A simple horse can be made with a little patience and imagination. Here are some easy directions for a corn-cob horse.

Cut the *dried corn cob* in pieces for the body, neck and head. Use the longest piece for the body and *drill* a hole in one end for a *dowel pin* to fit in. Drill another hole in the neck piece and attach the neck to the body piece by using *white glue* and the dowel pin.

Use the pointed end of a cob for the head, and attach this to the neck using the dowel pin, drill and white glue. Now drill holes for the dowel legs and fit dowels in carefully so the finished horse will stand up without wobbling. Use *corn silk* for the horse's mane and tail. Attach the silk with white glue. Ears and eyes may be made out of *felt*. A piece of *fabric* makes a good saddle blanket, and your corn cob horse is ready for display. Can you think of other animals to make?

GETTING SCIENTIFIC WITH CORN

Cut a kernel crosswise to see where it joins the cob. How does the cob serve as a store of nutrients for the kernel? The corn husks protect the corn kernels just as a blanket protects a new baby. Corn's worst enemy is wind. How does the stalk protect the ears? Can you find the meaning of the word node, pollen, tassel, and corn shock? Could you draw a diagram of a corn stalk marking all of the basic parts? What is the difference between popping corn, sweet corn and field corn?

GRANDMA'S PERFECT CORNBREAD

Most corn had to be ground before it could be used in cooking. The Indians showed the Pilgrims their method of grinding.

Sift 1 *cup white flour* with ¼ *cup white sugar*, 4 *teaspoons baking powder* and ½ *teaspoon salt*. Stir in 1 *cup corn meal*. Add 2 *eggs*, 1 *cup milk* and ¼ *cup softened shortening*. Beat this mixture with a *fork* for one minute. Pour into a *buttered pan* (9x9x2). Bake the cornbread at 425 degrees for twenty minutes. Use an iron corn stick pan to make individual corn treats. Fill each corn mold ⅔ full and bake at 425 degrees for twelve minutes. Try making cornbread in a greased Dutch oven over an open fire.

PILGRIM AND INDIAN HOMES

At the time of the first Thanksgiving there were seven homes built in the Plymouth Plantation. Their crude homes in America had many of the same features of their homes in England. They had clapboard sides and the children usually climbed a ladder to sleep in the lofts. Compare their homes to the native Indian huts. Did they both have windows? What materials were used for roofing?

In your Thanksgiving celebration you might make a miniature village showing the Indian huts and the Pilgrims' homes. Do some research and be authentic. (See Helpful Books—Thanksgiving.)

CHRISTMAS

History: The first known Christmas in America was recorded in the journals of Christopher Columbus in 1492. Many years later, the English settlers brought their Christmas customs with them from the mother country. Each settlement seemed to have its own special food, rituals, and social customs, but all were alike in this important aspect. Christmas was the time of giving and loving, and this tradition has lasted through the centuries. The pioneer children didn't have stores in which to buy gifts so they had to use the things they had around them. Where would they get a Christmas tree? How could they decorate it? What would they use for gifts? A pioneer Christmas had all of the ingredients of a marvelous holiday.

Traditions: To truly appreciate a pioneer Christmas one needs to do a quick study of some of the American traditions. The first recorded use of the Christmas tree in America was among the German settlers in Pennsylvania in 1746. The Dutch immigrants brought us St. Nicholas, the patron of holiday giving, and Dr. Clemet C. Moore gave the Saint real personality when he wrote the famous poem, "A Visit From St. Nicholas," which later became "The Night Before Christmas." Santa Claus with a sleigh pulled by eight tiny reindeer was first drawn by Thomas Nast in a cartoon showing Santa presenting gifts to the soldiers during the Civil War. Where has the tradition of greenery and holly come from? A study of pioneer customs can prove very interesting.

Decorations from Nature: Because there were no dime stores where children could buy glittery ornaments, they used their imaginations. They popped pop corn in long-handled wire baskets over the hot coals to use for stringing. To do this yourself, knot some *strong thread* and push the *needle* through the large part of the *popped corn. Cranberries* can be done in the same way and they add a beautiful color to the tree. *Walnut*

shells and *milk weed pods* turn into stars, butterflies and birds. A drum can be made from a *wooden spool,* and *pine cones* and *acorns* become little people. Here is how it is done.

The top few needles of a *short, fat, pine cone* are removed to make a place to *glue* the *round acorn.* The tip of the acorn becomes the person's nose, and eyes can be added with *a felt tip pen.* A *half circle* of *red felt* makes a cone shaped hat. A circle with a small wedge cut out makes a cape. Little women can be dressed with *calico aprons* and *lace scarves.* All parts of your acorn person can be put together with *white glue.* These can be used as decorations on the tree or in a nativity scene. Children can be made the same way using small pine cones and acorns.

Christmas Entertainment and Games: Since the pioneer children received few toys for Christmas, a great deal of the day was spent playing games and telling stories. The book, **It's Time for Christmas,** by Elizabeth Sechrist and Janet Woolsey contains some beautiful stories for Christmas. A progressive story is an exciting way to make up your own Christmas tale. Each person in the circle can add an event.

Part of the children's entertainment was helping to prepare Christmas goodies. Here is a delicious and easy recipe.

GINGERBREAD COOKIES

Combine ⅓ *cup brown sugar* and ⅓ *cup shortening.* Add ⅔ *cup molasses* and 1 *egg.* Sift together and add to the first mixture the following: 3 *cups sifted flour,* 1 *tablespoon baking powder,* 1 *teaspoon ginger* and ¼ *teaspoon salt.* Roll out this mixture and form into gingerbread people. Preheat the oven to 350 degrees and bake about six minutes. This makes twenty-four, four to six inch cookies. Cool and decorate them.

Many times the whole family joined in for a taffy pull. The directions for this are given in the Pioneer Cooking chapter.

After the meal time work was done, pioneer children still found time for games. A very old game used the holiday wreath as a target. It was suspended from the ceiling and the children would use balls of cotton batting or tissue-paper to throw through the wreath. The winner was the person getting the most "snowballs" through the wreath.

Can you think of some games that pioneer children could play? Many of the homes had two rooms, and dirt floors. Almost all the games needed to be played inside because of the snow.

Giving: Many of the first pioneer Christmases were celebrated with very few gifts. Here are a few of the gifts a child might have received in early America: marbles made by mother or brother out of hard cooked dough, a lump of pine gum to chew, a cuddly rag doll, or a doll made out of a wooden spoon. None of these was expensive, but they all contained a great deal of thoughtfulness and planning. A hand-made gift is still the most cherished today. Look through the chapters Toys and Dolls, and Games. Who would like to have one of your hand made-gifts? Sometimes there were no toys and no extra food, yet the pioneer children had a wonderful Christmas!

Helpful Books — Valentine's Day

Hearts, Cupids and Red Roses, Edna Barth, Seabury Press, 1974.

Valentine's Day, E. Guilfoile, Garrard Publishing, 1965.

Book of Holidays, J. Walker McSpadden, Crowell, 1958.

Fun with Greeting Cards, Joseph Leeming, Lippincott.

Helpful Books — Halloween

Witches, Pumpkins, and Grinning Ghosts, Edna Barth, Seabury Press, 1972.

Jack-o-Lantern, Edna Barth, Seabury Press, N.Y., 1974.

The Witch of Blackbird Pond, Elizabeth George Speare, Houghton Mifflin, 1958.

Mouskin's Golden House, Edna Miller, Prentice Hall, 1964.

Halloween, Helen Borten, Crowell, 1965.

Old Witch Rescues Halloween, Wende Devlin, Parents Magazine, 1972.

Helpful Books — Easter

All About American Holidays, Maymie R. Krythe, Harper and Brothers Publishers, N.Y., 1962.

A Holiday Book, Easter, Lillie Patterson, Garrard Publishing Co., Champaign, Ill., 1966.

Lillies, Rabbits, and Painted Eggs, Edna Barth, The Seabury Press, New York, 1970.

Helpful Books — Independence Day

Fourth of July, Charles P. Graves, Garrard Publishing Co., Champaign, Ill., 1963.

The Fourth of July Story, Alice Dalgliesh, Charles Scribner's and Sons, New York, 1956.

Your Flag and Mine, by Alice Curtis Desmond, The Macmillan Co., New York, 1960.

The American A. B. C., Maud and Miska Petersham, The Macmillan Company, N.Y., 1941.

Helpful Books—Apple Day

The Apple and Other Fruits, Millicent E. Selsam, Wm. Morrow & Co., N.Y.

The Apple and the Arrow, Mary and Conrad Buff, Houghton Mifflin Co., Boston.

The Story of Johnny Appleseed, by Aliki, Prentice-Hall, Inc.

Fruits We Eat, Caroll Lane Fenton and Herminie B. Kitchen, John Day Co., N.Y.

Helpful Books—Thanksgiving

The Thanksgiving Story, Alice Dalgliesh, Charles Scribners Sons, New York, 1954.

The First Thanksgiving, Lena Barksdale, Alfred A. Knopf, New York, 1954.

Thanksgiving Day, Robert Merrill Bartlett, Thomas Y. Crowell Company, New York, 1965.

Thanksgiving, Feast and Festival, Mildred Corell Luckhardt, Abingdon Press, Nashville, New York, 1966.

Early Settlers in America, Helene Hanff, Grosset and Dunlap, New York, 1965.

America Builds Homes, Alice Dalgliesh, Charles Scribners Sons, New York, 1938.

The First Book of the Early Settlers, Louise Dickinson Rich, Franklin Watts, Inc., New York, 1903.

Helpful Books—Christmas

The Book of Christmas Folklore, Tristram Coffin, The Seabury Press, N.Y., 1973.

American Christmas, Webster Schott, Robert Meyers, Hallmark Cards, K. C., Mo., 1965.

Christmas Holiday Book, Henderson, Miller, Gaden, Freed, Parents Magazine Press, N.Y.

The Secret of a Pioneer Christmas, Anderson Eddington, The Naturalist Publishing Co., 1972.

The Mice, the Monks and the Christmas Tree, George Selden, The Macmillan Company, New York, 1963.

The Forever Christmas Tree, Yoshiko Uchida, Schribner and Sons, New York, 1963.

The True Book of Holidays, John Wallace Purcell, Children's Press, Chicago.

Bits and Pieces

CANDLES

History: Candles were used primarily for light, but they were also used as timing devices by early American settlers who announced an event such as a prayer meeting by saying it would be at "early candlelight." The settlers realized that candles could be used to foretell the weather, too. When their flames snapped or burned with a dim light, rain and often wind would follow.

A colonial housewife never threw away any fat. She rendered it and stored it in pottery crocks. Candles were made of tallow with a wick down the center. Tallow, which is the hard fat from sheep, cows, or deer, sometimes had beeswax added to it to make it harder. The wick was made of spun flax or hemp. Later cotton wicks were used, and if nothing else was available, even the silk from milkweed was twisted into candle wicks.

One method of making candles was to pour hot wax into candle molds, which were made of hollow tin tubes fastened together. A second common method was to dip the wick many times in the hot wax letting the wax build up gradually. These candles were not made one at a time. Wicks were doubled, twisted, and hung on smooth wooden sticks called candle rods. Six or eight wicks were put on each rod. Two straight back chairs were set with the backs facing each other. Two long poles were placed parallel to each other across the backs of the chairs. The candle rods were laid across the poles like the rungs on a ladder. Boards were laid on the floor to catch any wax that dripped. This method is not hard to recreate today.

Procedure: You will need *two one-pound coffee cans*. Fill the first one with chunks of *parafin* (about five pounds for fifteen candles), and the second with *cold water*. Heat the parafin until it is all melted but not bubbling. Using *scissors* cut sections of *wired wick* eight to twelve inches long depending on the length of the candle you wish to make. Hold the top of the wick and dip it first into the can of parafin, then immediately into the can of cold water. The water cools the wax so that it builds up more quickly on the wick with repeated dipping. Continue dipping until your candle is the desired thickness. Younger children may find it easier and safer to tie the wick to the end of a stick and dip it while holding on to the other end. Broken crayons and old candles can be melted in the parafin can to give color to your candles.

ROSE POT POURRI

History: Before the event of aerosol room fresheners, people concocted their own favorite scents and preserved them in urns calling the mixture pot pourri. If a room smelled musty, the lady of the house stirred the rose petals and spices in the jar and left the lid off for awhile.

Procedure: Pick *rose petals* that have not fully bloomed and that are not wet from rain or dew. Place them on *paper* in a cool, dark spot indoors out of the direct sunlight. Move them around each day for several days until they have dried completely. Mix the petals in a *bowl* with ½ ounce of violet scented *talcum powder,* ½ teaspoon of *cinnamon,* and ½ teaspoon of *cloves*. Put all of this by layers in a tightly closed container with a teaspoon of *salt* sprinkled over each layer. Then during the winter open the jar for a breath of summer.

Related Activities:
1. A method of preserving meat through the winter

was to salt it. The rose petals in this recipe are salted to help preserve them. Can you do any experiments to discover what makes salt a preservative?

STENCILING

History: Stencil decorating was introduced into England during the 1600's and became popular in America during Andrew Jackson's time. Stenciling was done on chairs, beds, chests, tables and trays. At this time a professional stenciler was as popular as a tanner or cooper. A stencil is merely an object or design cut into paper. This is then placed over an article (wood, tin, or glass) and the opening is painted. For fancy designs silver and gold powders were added to highlight certain parts of the design. Doorways and ceiling moldings were often accented in beautiful 1850 homes by a repetitive stencil design.

Procedure: Draw or trace your pattern on *tracing paper*. Then transfer your design to *light weight tag board* or *heavy construction paper*. With *scissors* or *mat* knife cut out the design you have decided on. This becomes your pattern. The pattern can be dipped in a thin layer of paraffin to help it keep its shape and this also enables you to use the pattern over and over. Be sure and leave a large border around your cut-out design. There are several ways to get your desired effect. You may trace the opening of your stencil, remove the pattern, and fill in your lines, or you may merely lay the stencil down on the background material and paint over all the open areas. Stenciling can be done on fabric, paper, wood, glass or tin. It might be best to start on paper or wood to get the feel of it.

Related Activities:
1. A beautiful and very simple pattern can be made by folding a piece of light weight tag board and cutting

along the fold. Children will delight in opening up their folded paper to see their creations!

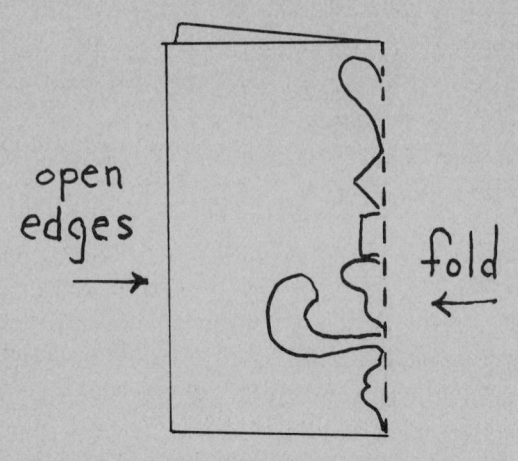

open edges → fold ←

2. Some fancy stenciling was done with metallic powders. The powders were applied to a sticky varnish. This more delicate process is explained in an excellent book entitled, **Early American Crafts and Hobbies,** written by Raymond and Marguerite W. Yates.

SOAP-MAKING

History: It is easy to imagine the beginnings of soap-making. As fat meat was cooked on outdoor fires, the melted fat would drip onto the potash material on the bottom of the fire where it formed into clumps of soap-like material when cooled. Ashes alone had been used for centuries for cleaning and polishing and this "soap" was discovered to be even better.

While America was being settled, homemakers had to know how to make their own soap because it was not readily available in stores. The ingredients of homemade soap are pure and good for your skin. This soap is an excellent treatment for poison ivy. You can use your favorite oils or scents to personalize your recipe.

Procedure: Heat your soap mixture in *enamel* or *iron containers* and use *wooden spoons* for stirring. A *cardboard box lid* lined with *wax paper* may be used for a mold. The hardened soap is cut into bars. Today it is possible to use individual size plastic containers for molds if you wish. The following recipe makes about six ounces of soap which is enough for two small bars or one cake if using a plastic margarine bowl.

Clean your old *grease* by boiling it with two parts *water*. Measure ½ cup of warm fat into a plastic container. In another container measure ¼ cup of cool water. Add 1 tablespoon of *lye** to the water and stir with a wooden spoon. Then add the lye water to the fat while stirring. Stir until it is as thick as honey. Add a teaspoon of perfume if you like, and pour into a mold. Cover it and let it set twenty-four hours. Remove from the mold and let the soap dry for two weeks.

*Remember to be very careful when you mix the lye and water together. Until it is mixed with warm grease, the lye solution is harmful to your skin and the fumes are harmful to breathe. This step should be done outside or with good ventilation inside.

CRYSTALIZED VIOLETS

Violets can add beauty as well as vitamin C to your menu. Wash the flower, coat it in *egg white* and dip it in *granulated sugar*. When the petals are dry and firm they may be eaten as candy or used to decorate cakes or ice cream.

GEORGE'S PEACH STICKS

To give cake batter a delicate peach flavor, cut twigs from a peach tree when they are full of sap in the Spring. Bruise the ends. Use these to beat the batter. This was George Washington's favorite flavoring for cakes.

HOME COMFORTS

To get rid of a *sore throat,* blow sulphur through a goose quill on the throat.

Fill your *wet boots* with dry oats for a few hours to keep the leather from shrinking.

Rust stains can be removed by bringing rhubarb juice to a boil and soaking the material in the solution.

To make your own *furniture polish,* use this recipe:

>One-half pint linseed oil
>One-half pint vinegar
>One-half pint turpentine

(Linseed oil is available in hardware stores.)

If you have *blisters* from breaking in your new shoes, try this carrot salve:

>Scrape two carrots and stew in two tablespoons hog's lard. Add two plantain leaves. Strain.

If you have trouble with *peanut butter sticking* to the roof of your mouth, turn the bread upside down before eating it!

NOTES

NOTES

NOTES

NOTES

NOTES

NOTES